Group Leadership
A Manual for Group Counseling Leaders

Second Edition

Marilyn Bates,
late of California State University, Fullerton

Clarence D. Johnson,
Anne Arundel Public Schools, Maryland

Kenneth E. Blaker,
University of Santa Clara

LOVE PUBLISHING COMPANY
Denver · London

ACKNOWLEDGMENT

Marilyn Bates' commitment to humanity lives through her publications, as well as through those who worked with her in the many areas of her daily life. As a self-recognized student of life and as a professionally-recognized contributor to counseling, Marilyn influenced great numbers of people directly and indirectly. It is with conviction that we acknowledge her the way she preferred — as a professional contributor to the betterment of humanity.

C. D. Johnson
Kenneth E. Blaker

Copyright © 1982 Love Publishing Company

Printed in the U.S.A.
ISBN 0-89108-105-4
Library of Congress Catalog Card Number 81-81524
10 9 8 7 6 5 4

Preface

The first edition of this book appeared at a time (1972) when the use of group processes in public schools and institutions was suspect. The intent of the first edition was to clarify the group leader's responsibilities to group members and to clearly define the group leader competencies (knowledges, skills, attitudes) necessary to fulfill those responsibilities. This edition maintains the same purpose and, therefore, the same assumptions, standards, and convictions.

If the *assumption* is correct that experience as a group member is a necessary *and sufficient* preparation for group leadership, this book need not exist. The authors believe that the above assumptions are incorrect, misleading, and antithetical to responsible group leadership.

It is the position of the writers that, while group membership is a necessary preparation for group leadership, it is *not* sufficient in itself. We believe that the experience of group membership is essentially different from the experience of group leadership because the former requires an intense focusing on self, while the latter requires an intense loosening — almost abnegation — of self. The group member looks inward and relates outward; the group leader looks outward and relates inward. The cognitive and emotional processes inherent in the two roles are quite different from each other, and while we believe that being a member is essential preparation for being a leader, we also see it as only that — preparatory.

Further, it is our firm *conviction* that group leadership can and must be taught. The group leader must have the professional tools that will enable him or her to activate group processes in a way that ensures that members have growth-producing experiences. The main focus of this book is to present such tools. The theoretical constructs that provide the rationale from which the tools are derived are embodied in the EXTENSIONAL GROUP MODEL.

The extensional group model is founded in existential philosophy, which holds constant specific leadership responsibilities. These responsibilities assure optimum group member opportunity to explore choices to lead to greater degrees of personal freedom. These responsibilities have been extrapolated into group leadership competencies. The material in this book is directed toward this leadership knowledge, skill, and attitude.

Also, the material presented herein is directed toward the leader concerned with people who are "well" and want to get better or grow to greater degrees of personal freedom. In turn, the paradigm presented in this book is a "well model" rather than a "remedial model." Consequently, it is appropriate for leaders who work within institutional settings (public schools, probation departments, mental health units, etc.), as well as those who work outside of institutional settings (marriage counseling groups, family counseling groups, church-related groups, and so on).

Chapters 9 and 10 contain totally new material devoted to examining some of the various settings in which extensional groups are known to have been effective. The personal benefit derived from participating in such groups is the learning that results from studying one's own behavior, the behavior of others, and the interactive behavior during various individual and group activities. These benefits are available to group participants regardless of their age or their social milieu.

C. D. J.
K. E. B.

Contents

v

Figures

1

The Extensional Group Model

The Extensional Group Model

The Extensional Group Model

1

In our group work we have operated on the assumption that open, honest, direct communication among human beings is both possible and desirable. Relatively closed, inhibited, and self-protective styles of interpersonal behavior often seem more common, but we consider such styles to be undesirable and even emotionally unhealthy.

Almost all our efforts as group leaders have been directed toward protecting the rights of individual group members and maintaining a group environment in which members are willing, if not eager, to risk self-disclosure, to reveal their thoughts, feelings, and reactions as they are experiencing them. In such an environment, group members are more inclined to relate to each other as they *really* are, rather than as they think they *ought* to be. They feel relatively less inhibited, and they feel less need to present a protective or defensive facade. Spontaneous interaction of this nature is not only the goal of the group leader but also the substance and essence of the extensional group process. Group interaction is most beneficial to members when it is spontaneous. Both educational and therapeutic benefits can be derived from group experiences that are carefully designed to lead to greater spontaneity. Through such experiences individual group members can learn new ways of perceiving themselves and others.

Groups can be "for better" or "for worse." Although it is inconceivable that a leader would deliberately set out to form a group for the worse, the literature from all disciplines dealing with interaction groups indicates that some group experiences do diminish or almost destroy their members (Eddy & Lubin, 1971; Howard, 1970; Shostrom, 1970; Yalom & Lieberman, 1971). Participants may approach interaction groups anticipating one type of experience and find something quite different.

As a result of reports of "for worse" group experiences, the public and mental health professionals alike have become cautious in their expectations about the benefits that group interaction can provide (Goldberg, 1970). It is highly probable that many people who could use group processes for positive growth avoid getting involved in them for fear of a destructive experience. Yet groups *can* be "for better." In the hands of an adequately trained leader, participants need not fear a destructive experience, but can anticipate positive growth. Competent leaders are the key.

Training group leaders to handle group processes so that members have a positive experience is the focus of this book. Such training involves both theory and practice. Chapters 1-3 present the philosophical and theoretical framework of the extensional group model, as contrasted with the remedial group model. Chapters 4-10 describe the practice derived from the philosophy and theory.

TWO MODELS OF GROUP

The group model that provides the conceptual framework for this book is termed "extensional group." The extensional (growth) group, which is based on a "well model," is contrasted with a remedial (therapeutic) group model.

The remedial and extensional group models are presented in order to delineate clearly (1) two types of interaction experiences that differ both in purpose and process, and (2) the theoretical stance of the authors of this book. The remedial group is mainly a *therapy* group, which is based on a medical model and is primarily motivated by the deficiency needs of members. The extensional group is seen as a *self-actualizing* group, which is based on a developmental conceptualization and is motivated primarily by the growth needs of members.

Other kinds of groups (e.g., guidance groups in schools) may have some of the characteristics of group work described in this book. We have elected, however, to focus on *extensional* groups and how they may be beneficial in a wide range of group settings. The various settings are described briefly in this chapter and in greater detail in Chapters 9 and 10.

The Remedial (Therapy) Model

Much confusion seems to exist about groups that are formed for what is essentially the remediation of inadequate personal functioning and groups that are formed for *extending adequate personality functioning.* Ill people need to get better. Well people also can get better. Remedial groups are concerned with ill persons who are not currently coping with the stresses and strains of living. The group leader conducting a remedial group may find that members must regress before they can mobilize their positive growth forces. Members may need to "act out" their hostilities in infantile fashion before they can release nonhostile forces. They may need to vent angers, fears, and hates exhaustively before they are able to express love, caring, and hope. Indeed, this type of group does need to "work through" much negative content before positive content can surface.

The mistake many group leaders have made is to assume that all groups must regress to more primitive forms of behavior before growth forces can be activated. Traditionally, leaders have assumed that *all* members must discharge energies connected with experiences charged with hate, fear, and anger. The initial group sessions, then, were necessarily directed toward eliciting expressions of irrational, id-based, infantile behaviors. Once this cycle was completed, members could move on to explore new ways of behaving that were more mature, rational, and ego-based.

That regression is necessary and appropriate in remedial groups is recognized. Groups composed of members who need to repair personality defects must scrape off layers of debilitating defense mechanisms before the core of personality can be restructured even minimally. Leaders of remedial, regressive groups — the psychiatrist, the psychotherapist, the clinical psychologist — require training in the medical model.

Although the emphasis of this book is on the extensional model, readers may benefit from an illustration of what we consider a remedial group.

Robin Gilbert (van Stone & Gilbert, 1974), a psychiatric social worker at the Veterans Administration Hospital in Menlo

Park, California, uses group interaction as a primary therapeutic mode. His patients are veterans who are experiencing serious psycho-social problems, particularly in the area of drug and alcohol abuse. The group is used as a forum in which patients' mental defenses are repeatedly attacked by fellow patients. Gilbert's groups are patterned after the Synanon Games, although in their present form they have some features unique to Gilbert's leadership style.

In Gilbert's groups an underlying thesis is that a person's unhappy life situation cannot change for the better until the person confronts his or her present situation honestly, rather than projecting blame on others or justifying present disruptive behavior. Group members vigorously and savagely attack each other's attempts to defend or justify their own behavior. Short of physical assault, the attacks are relentless and personal. The language and accusations are voiced in the roughest terms imaginable. Sometimes a patient is forcibly restrained, say, on a mattress, by several fellow patients, while struggling for freedom. The group sessions are dramatic, to say the least.

Gilbert's remedial groups do provide physical warmth and support when patients gain constructive insight into their problems or live up to promises that they indeed will do something constructive about their predicaments. In addition to the assaults, an abundance of positive reinforcement comes in the form of hugs and caring words when progress warrants it.

The Extensional (Growth) Model

The traditional notion that groups are primarily for ill people, entailing a regressive, acting-out, remedial process initially in *all* groups, is outmoded. The point of view of this book is that groups *can* serve another function, extending the life-space of members by extending their capabilities even if they are currently functioning at a satisfactory or even self-actualizing level of existence. This particular use of groups has been confused with the remedial use of groups. A differentiation of procedures is mandated for the two types of groups. This chapter specifies differences in assumptions and procedures between a remedial group and an extensional group.

The extensional group model begins with the assumption that *well people can get better,* and the group is one arena where this can occur. The extensional group focuses on the concept that even people who are functioning adequately, who are fairly comfortable in interpersonal relationships, who may be coping with the demands of daily living, can still experience growth in a self-actualizing paradigm. Although members of this type of group are "well" rather than "ill," they want to get *better.* They want to enhance their learning ability; want to attain more enjoyment from living; want more spontaneity, more creativity, more autonomy, more acceptance of necessary restrictions, more joy, more productivity, more awareness and acceptance of themselves and others. In short, they want to accelerate the process of self-actualization.

The extensional group provides an opportunity for members to explore more satisfying ways of behaving in relation to self and in relation to one another. The life-space of each member can be examined thoroughly without threat of this life-space being diminished. The life-spaces of members as they interface can also be explored without fear of negation.

The extensional group model anticipates that members will leave each session and the group experience itself augmented rather than diminished. Through the group experience each member extends facets of his or her personality and strengths in growth directions. This model is developmental rather than remedial, extensional rather than regressive. The leader, then, does not assume that negative forces must be siphoned off before positive forces can be manifest. The leader can begin at the growth stations of members and move on, rather than, as in the remedial group, encourage members to regress to earlier forms of behavior with the intent of working through or minimizing blocks to development. Each member can begin on the base that "I'm okay, you're okay" (Harris, 1969) and proceed to develop specifics to elaborate that stance.

The remedial group is conceptualized as operating mainly on a negative pole, dealing with negative content such as hate relationships, anger toward authority figures, resentment of early experiences, debilitating defense mechanisms — in general, behaviors that are primarily based in a more primitive ego state. Leaders of remedial groups have to be prepared to deal with many negative forces, and they find that one negative comment tends to generate others. Negative elements in the group cause others to emerge, which, in turn, trigger additional negative interaction. Thus, the initial content of the group interaction may focus on potentially destructive elements.

In the extensional group, leaders deal primarily with positive forces. One positive force tends to generate another. The positive elements in these groups incubate others, activating a positively reinforcing cycle.

These two types of groups overlap to some extent. The remedial group does process positive forces, although the leader's mental set is alert to negative forces. The extensional group deals with a proportion of negative content, but it has a predominant mind set for attending to positive forces. Figure 1.1 provides a diagram for these two types of groups. Note that

FIGURE 1.1
Two Group Models

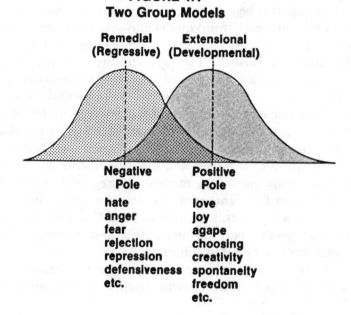

Remedial   Extensional
(Regressive) (Developmental)

Negative Pole	Positive Pole
hate	love
anger	joy
fear	agape
rejection	choosing
repression	creativity
defensiveness	spontaneity
etc.	freedom
	etc.

where the groups overlap, the remedial group contains positive content, and the extensional gains negative content. The diagram illustrates the proportionate amount of negative or positive content that is likely to exist initially in either type of group.

In either group setting, remedial or extensional, the success of the group's interaction depends upon the degree of trust, openness, and interpersonal risk-taking among group members. Members who reveal little of themselves cannot be expected to benefit from their group experience to the same extent as members who are open and sharing.

BENEFITS TO BE DERIVED
FROM EXTENSIONAL GROUPS

When we look at the people and events around us — even when we look at ourselves in the mirror — we can never escape the possibility that what we see is a subjective view filtered through a storehouse of past experiences. Hearing from others about their perceptions and observations can confirm or contradict what we think we already know. Their sharing can give us bits of information of which we may have been unaware, all contributing to a more clearly defined picture of who and what we are and the kinds of options offered by people and events about us.

Those of us who desire a clearer, more accurate picture of ourselves should have an opportunity to focus on ourselves and our personal value systems. Are our expressed values consistent with our behaviors? Group interaction affords us an opportunity to find out. The feedback we receive from fellow group members can give us information to which we might not otherwise have access.

A minister in a group of graduate students had commented that his love for mankind was unconditional and universal. He had chosen the ministry to be able to express his love through service. Several group members shared with him their reservations, as they had been the target of his wrath when they had challenged an earlier opinion of his. At that time the minister had acted defensively and with hostility, which suggested that maybe his love for mankind wasn't unconditional as he had claimed.

The minister started to protest, only to catch himself doing the very thing they had mentioned. He paused reflectively and with a slight grin replied, "Now *that's* an eye opener."

Two rather complex processes are involved in identifying and clarifying self. One is the self-investigation that hopefully results in self-knowledge; the other is personal decision making based upon self-knowledge. To be able to adopt behavior consistent with our value system, we must know and accept ourselves. At this point of knowing ourselves, we must make decisions. Either we act according to the values we profess and discard values that no longer have meaning for us or we ignore the inconsistencies. But having a source of feedback about how consistent we are is useful.

Personal benefits are available through the group process regardless of the setting or purpose of the group. Feedback and collective reasoning can be tremendously productive, especially when compared with the information and reasoning capabilities of one person alone. At times, of course, group efforts exerted to achieve a task or solve a problem are paralytic because individuals within the group have concealed motives. Perhaps certain group members have competitive or disruptive intentions rather than a willingness to share and cooperate. In such a situation a skillful group leader can facilitate a cooperative spirit that will develop the creative rather than the destructive potential of the group.

LEVELS OF SELF-DISCLOSURE

> *So often, that which we are is sacrificed*
> *to that which we wish ourselves to be.*
> *(Anglund, 1970)*

Why do many of us seem to be so inhibited, protective, and defensive about disclosing our present (here and now) feelings to each other? *Why Am I Afraid To Tell You Who I Am?* (Powell, 1969) is a little book that asks a tremendously provocative question. How many of us can truthfully deny that we spend a good part of our lives trying to be the kind of person we think we *ought* to be rather than the kind of person we really *are?* Think of that for a moment. So many roles are expected of us, so many roles that we are obliged to fulfill. We are fathers, mothers, friends, neighbors, teachers, counselors, students, affiliates of organizations and churches. We believe that certain behaviors and attitudes are expected of us as part of the roles in which we are engaged. That is the way of life.

We are not suggesting that expected roles are inappropriate or undesirable. On the contrary, to be contributing members of society we must be conscious of the need for our roles as a part of family, school, community, and nation. But the point is that we are often inclined to *play* roles rather than be ourselves as a part of the roles. You can probably recall events in your life when you were so conscious of the roles in which you were functioning that you knowingly suppressed your own thoughts and attitudes in order to maintain the image that you perceived to be consistent with your role. A good example of this is the teacher who struggles through an answer to a student's question when the most honest response would be, "I don't know" or 'I'm not certain."

A young, first-year physical education teacher was supervising a basketball relay race. In his first year as a teacher, he had made a special effort to be a model of masculinity — strong, consistent, purposeful, emotionless. Everything, including basketball relay races, was to be taken very seriously.

Each boy dribbled his ball to the opposite end of the court for a layup, then returned to half court, where he passed the ball to a waiting teammate. Excitement was high and the noise deafening as the boys cheered and encouraged their teammates. The last boy on the team that was headed for victory had just released the ball as the teacher started across the court, blowing his whistle to stop the game and announce that the winning team would not have to run laps.

The runner-up team was close behind the winning team, and their last man had let go of his ball in a bullet-like pass just a split second behind the winning pass. The ball hit the teacher's head, caroming high in the air. There was a sudden, startled silence as the boys looked in disbelief. But the teacher continued walking, not even acknowledging the incident with a wince and with only the slightest interruption of his whistle blowing. Maintaining his masculine self-image was too important to him to admit to pain, embarrassment, or wavering purpose.

Jourard's (1971) chapter entitled "Lethal Aspects of the Male Role" contains a message of importance for anyone of either sex. We often present a "front" or facade that we want others to see and believe. Our behavior is adjusted in a way we think consistent with the image we wish to convey. Often the facade does not match our feelings and true attitudes. At these times there is an incongruency between our presented self and our "real" self. When our presented self and our real self are reasonably congruent, we can think of ourselves as being *authentic*. The reader can imagine the discrepancy between what must have been occurring in the physical education teacher's real self and the image he was presenting to the students.

The difference between the presented self and the real self is far more complex than the simple dichotomy described so far. Depending upon the environment we are in or the company around us, we vary in our willingness and ability to be authentic. A helpful way of conceptualizing the complexity of our varying degrees of authenticity is to think of the structural characteristics of an onion. The outer layer of an onion is quite different in texture and color from the layers near the center. As each layer is peeled away, a tender, more vulnerable surface is exposed. In our personalities our facades are often a protection for what we consider the more vulnerable and sensitive, yet more real and authentic parts of ourselves.

Behavior is authentic when what we say and do is congruent with what we are really thinking and feeling. This, of course, is clearly a matter of degree rather than a state of being. When we say that someone is authentic or genuine, we mean that he or she seems authentic and genuine most of the time we are with him or her. Even the most authentic people, though, find it expedient sometimes not to disclose exactly what they are thinking or feeling.

Examine the model in Figure 1.2. We have borrowed it from Lewis and Streitfeld (1970) and Simon, Howe, and Kirschenbaum (1972) and have adapted it as a pictorial description of our "onion" concept. It provides us another way of looking at personal authenticity.

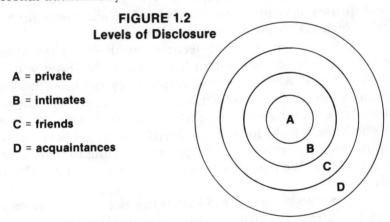

FIGURE 1.2
Levels of Disclosure

A = private

B = intimates

C = friends

D = acquaintances

Consider the degrees of self-disclosure we are willing to allow. By self-disclosure we do not mean the revelation of intimate or personal details from our lives. Self-disclosure need not be synonymous with bringing skeletons out of the family closet. We can begin to *know* another person without necessarily knowing a lot *about* the person. To us, self-disclosure means revealing the present state of one's feelings and thoughts — saying it like it is *when* it is. In gestalt language it is being

13

and speaking in the *here and now*. The more inclined we are to trust the people around us, the more inclined we are to reveal honestly what is happening within us at a given moment, whether the revelation is positive or negative. This type of self-disclosure allows one to be known to others.

At the "D" level in Figure 1.2 we would place the kind of self-disclosure that is relatively "safe." It includes conversational types of interaction and disclosure. "D" level also includes the facades we present when we are consciously behaving in a manner consistent with a role we wish to project. Conscious role-consistent behaviors do not normally carry the trust necessary for sharing ourselves authentically. "D" level can also be a protective shell when we do not want others to know what is really going on within us. When we are feeling defensive or vulnerable, we engage in a host of behaviors that do not match our inner feelings. The "D" level of self-disclosure is typical when one first enters a group, but most group members easily and quickly develop a sense of belonging and are willing to relinquish "D"-level attitudes and behaviors.

"C"-level thoughts and feelings are those we would feel comfortable in sharing with a friend but perhaps not with an acquaintance. And we would comfortably disclose "B"-level thoughts to someone with whom we are intimate, but not to a friend or acquaintance. Then there is the private area ("A" level) we all have. It is the locus of our belief system, our basic values. It includes thoughts and feelings we are willing to share with a selective few. We may choose not to share parts of the "A" level with anyone.

Using this model, group leaders can assess their hypotheses of what is really occurring within group members by comparing it with behavior observed and the words heard. The leader's task is to create and maintain a trusting environment in the group, one in which facades ("D" level) seem less necessary, and inhibitions that limit disclosure are reduced. "C" level, and maybe even "B" level, may be revealed and explored. The group leader's duty, however, is to protect the member's right to privacy, which is inviolate in the extensional model. Despite the similarity in appearance between Figure 1.2 and a bull's-eye, the private "A" area is *not* the target. Disclosure that is volunteered is more in keeping with our positive approach to extensional group work.

PENETRATING THE PROTECTIVE SHELL

"Penetrating" the protective shell may sound overly assertive, but that is not our intention. By "penetration" we suggest that the leader's function is to exert an influence on the group's environment that will free members to trust each other enough to open themselves and let themselves be known to each other. If the leader is successful in helping dissolve or moving through the "D"-level protective, defensive facades, his or her group goal of personal growth for group members should be accomplished.

John Wallen, in his article, "The Constructive Use of Feelings" (n.d.), asks his readers to engage in an experiment over the course of several days. The task is to examine the way in which people talk about feelings. Expressions like, "Now let's keep our feelings out of this," or "You shouldn't feel that way" are certainly common experiences for people engaged in problem-solving dialogue. Crying often prompts a response like, "Don't cry," "You'll feel better," "Cheer up," or "It's ridiculous to feel that way." An expression of anger might be met with the admonishment, "You're letting your feelings get the best of you" or the assertion, "You can't behave like that."

These statements surely indicate an attitude about feelings that is familiar to all of us. When we understand that some people are naturally unaccustomed to or uncomfortable about dealing directly with reports of their feelings and the feelings of others, we become sensitive to the delicate balance of the group dynamic process. In this process, with its underlying assumption that self-disclosure is an essential condition for developing self-awareness, we encourage group members to risk that which they have protected so well.

If we are to proceed into this protected life-space, we must take care not to violate that which is private and personal. As leaders or members of a group, we must recognize that one of the most cherished and sacred rights within our society is that of privacy. Humankind has waged both personal and general battle to protect this right. A person whose private space is

15

invaded usually reacts as would a nation whose boundaries have been attacked. In many ways the life-space we protect is analogous to territorial boundaries that animals protect. When our privacy is violated, we react defensively. Thus, it becomes essential within the group setting to be sensitive to a person's private world and to allow him or her to maintain privacy if he or she chooses to do so.

This maxim appears easy to respect — deceptively so. In the pursuit of the dynamic upon which group counseling is based (sharing of self), invasion of privacy becomes a tempting modus operandi not only for the leader but for other members as well. All too often in our zeal to pursue members' inner feelings, trying to help them express themselves in hopes that they will learn more about themselves, we use probing and pressure to force self-disclosure, rather than allowing it to happen. As a result, members whose personal space have been violated are likely to react defensively, either by investing more in maintaining their facades or by withdrawing and becoming more inhibited and guarded. Individuals who feel their privacy being invaded will be unwilling to venture outside the protective barrier.

Guaranteeing one's right to privacy is founded on our respect for the individual. It also serves as a firm reminder that extensional group work is not intended by design to be psychotherapeutic. On the basis of our experience in group work with adults and children, we maintain that penetration of the protective shell is essential for development of self-awareness, but, ironically, the concept of penetration usually raises images of intrusion or attack from the outside.

Our model of group counseling is best exemplified by thinking of an egg about to hatch. An egg has a protective shell. Inside the shell is an unborn chick. With the proper external conditions the chick will penetrate the shell and emerge at precisely the most beneficial moment. We would not break the shell prematurely. When the shell is naturally penetrated from within, the conditions for growth have been maximized.

One of the group leader's *primary functions*, then, is to protect individual members' rights. When they feel certain that the group milieu will be "safe," they will be more inclined to emerge from their protective shells by sharing their here-and-now experiences.

Jim, a graduate student, was an inhibited group member who appeared suspicious of his group leader's motives. When the leader suggested that the group do a "mill-in" game to better understand the concept of personal space, Jim bombarded the leader with questions about the activity's purpose and worth. Although Jim had not expressed his opposition, he obviously was not looking forward to participating in the "mill-in."

As the group milled aimlessly with their eyes closed, Jim "milled" directly to a corner, where he remained facing the wall. When the group returned to the circle to discuss their experiences, several members pressed Jim for an explanation of his behavior. At first he claimed that he "just happened" to end up in a corner. Several group members challenged that statement and continued pressing for an explanation they could accept as credible. Finally Jim said, "I'd rather not talk about this any more."

A dissatisfied member confronted Jim with the incongruency of his words and his behavior. The leader intervened, reminding the group that Jim had expressed his desire to be left alone and that it should be honored.

Several sessions later, Jim, whose participation had been increasing, volunteered that he had been afraid of the "mill-in" game because he might have "bumped up against a girl," which would have embarrassed him tremendously. His escape to the corner was an effort to avoid the possibility of embarrassment.

All of us have protective shells. Leaders who are able to relinquish the "D" level in order to express themselves authentically in the here and now, while not invading the more private levels of group members, have a good start toward implementing group techniques and strategies effectively.

EXTENSIONAL GROUP MODEL SETTINGS

Before proceeding to Chapter 2, in which we will examine the philosophical base of extensional groups, it might be helpful to consider briefly the types of groups that seem to benefit from this approach. Although the philosophical base influences several common aspects of leader conduct and use of facilitative techniques, the group setting and the specific group purpose dictate the appropriateness and intensity of participant interaction. Not *all* techniques and *all* degrees of interaction intensity are appropriate for *all* types of extensional groups. Furthermore, group leaders may not be aware of the extensional model and, therefore, do not identify their approach as such. The various group settings to be described are, by design, neither guidance groups nor remedial groups. Thus, by our definition, they can be described as extensional groups because the processes and techniques employed are intended to help individuals capitalize on the growth potential they already possess. Details of group organization and suggestions for appropriate techniques are forthcoming in Chapters 8 and 9. Here, we wish to provide only a brief overview of the wide range of settings in which extensional groups have proved beneficial.

Educational Settings

The mention of "group" work among educators at one time automatically triggered negative feelings and resistance. This reaction was partly a carryover effect from a time when *group* experience usually meant something on the order of sensitivity or encounter groups. Verbal assaults on group members and attempts to strip away psychological defenses were frightening prospects that seemed to characterize popular conceptions of what groups were about. Newspaper and media reports of nude encounters, suicides, mental breakdowns, divorces, and similar negative outcomes of group experiences gave justification for being cautious when assessing the value of such activities in an educational setting.

Extensional groups *can* be used effectively as an educational procedure. At all levels of education, teachers, instructors, and professors are expressing a growing interest in finding ways to help their students identify and explore their values. Values clarification is a vital part of personal decision making. Developing interpersonal skills and learning how to express feelings constructively are other areas of emerging educational interest. The extensional model provides an effective framework for implementing these nonacademic concerns, although age, maturity, and grade level are obviously determinants as to *how* it is to be implemented.

Community Settings

Women's groups, shelters for runaways, half-way houses, senior citizens' groups, church groups, and juvenile probation groups are examples of the types of community settings in which extensional group work is proving effective. Typically, such groups have been assembled for the purpose of instructing and informing. The goals of these groups are usually noble, but the *method* of implementing them is usually inefficient. Instead of developing a commitment to their own welfare and betterment, participants often become passive recipients of information and advice.

Groups designed from the extensional model, however, seem to overcome much of the passivity. A group environment in which individuals state their views and then are afforded feedback, suggestions, and ideas from their peers seems far more motivating for self-responsibility and positive action than the typical didactic situation in which someone of "authority" tells participants what is good for them.

Medical Settings

The growing interest in holistic health encompasses the idea that patients can influence the outcome of their own medical predicaments. Whether the medical setting is intended for temporary, chronic, or terminal patients and their families, the type of group interaction encouraged from the extensional model is proving helpful in reducing the sense of isolation and despair often experienced in hospice-type settings, convalescent homes, rehabilitation centers, and pain-control centers.

19

Discovering that others suffer from a similar affliction or condition decreases the "why me?" feeling. Also, receiving support and suggestions from those who truly understand as a result of *their* situations adds a richer dimension to empathy. Traditionally, group work conducted in medical settings has been exclusively remedial. Now, the emerging interest in group work for holistic health purposes is new and exciting.

SUMMARY

Chapter 1 introduced the extensional (growth) model for group work and contrasted it with the remedial (therapy) model. The extensional model focuses on what is "right" about an individual rather than trying to correct something that has gone "wrong." A basic assumption of the extensional model is that benefits derived from self-disclosure and subsequent feedback from group members will encourage self-responsibility and personal development.

The group, influenced by competent leadership, is a unique and safe environment for self-disclosure. Self-disclosure should always be by a member's choice, and the leader has a responsibility to protect each member's right to privacy. Even though the model stresses the importance of self-disclosure, it is equally important that the member *choose* to self-disclose.

Chapter 1 concludes with a brief preview of various group settings — educational, community, and medical — in which the extensional model is known to have been effective. These are discussed further in Chapters 9 and 10.

REFERENCES

Anglund, Joan Walsh. *A Slice of Snow*. New York: Harcourt, Brace, Jovanovich, 1970.

Eddy, William B., and Lubin, Bernard. "Laboratory Training and Encounter Groups," *Personnel and Guidance Journal*, Vol. 49, No. 8 (April 1971), pp. 625-34.

Goldberg, Carl. *Encounter: Group Sensitivity Training Experience.* New York: Science House, 1970.

Harris, Thomas. *I'm OK, You're OK.* New York: Harper and Row, 1969.

Howard, Jane. *Please Touch.* New York: McGraw-Hill, 1970.

Jourard, Sidney. *The Transparent Self.* Rev. ed. New York: Van Nostrand Reinhold, 1971.

Lewis, Howard R., and Streitfeld, Harold S. *Growth Games: How to Tune into Yourself, Your Family, Your Friends.* New York: Harcourt, Brace, Jovanovich, 1970.

Powell, John. *Why Am I Afraid to Tell You Who I Am?* Chicago: Argus Publications, 1969.

Shostrom, Everett L. "Group Therapy: Let the Buyer Beware," in *Readings in Psychology Today.* Del Mar, CA: CRM Books, 1970, pp. 149-51.

Simon, Sidney, Howe, Leland W., and Kirschenbaum, Howard. *Values Clarification: A Handbook of Practical Strategies for Teachers and Students.* New York: Hart Publishing Co., 1972.

van Stone, William W., and Gilbert, Robert P. "Peer Confrontation Groups," in Jules Masserman (Ed.), *Current Psychiatric Therapies.* New York: Grune and Stratton, 1974.

Wallen, John. *The Constructive Use of Feelings.* Beaverton, OR: Tektronix, Inc., n.d.

Yalom, Irvin, and Lieberman, M. "Sensitivity Training: Caveat Emptor," *Behavior Today,* Vol. 2, No. 21, May 24, 1971.

2

The Philosophical Base
of the Extensional Group Model

- Existentialist Concept: Existence Precedes Essence
- Existence Precedes Essence: Implications for an Extensional Group
    The Essence of the Group Leader
    Making Choices in an Extensional Group
- Existentialist Concept: Humankind Is Condemned to Freedom
- Humankind Is Condemned to Freedom: Implications for an Extensional Group
    The Existentialist Paradox and Human Nourishment
    Existential Freedom and the Question of Values
- Existentialist Concept: One Defines Self Through One's Actions and Only Through One's Actions
- One Defines Self Through One's Actions: Implications for an Extensional Group
- Existentialist Concept: The Encounter — The "I - Thou" Relationship Defines Group Processes and Content
- The Encounter: Implications for an Extensional Group
- Summary

2

The Philosophical Base
of the Extensional Group Model

The philosophical foundation of the extensional group is the *existentialist* framework. The implications of existentialism for individual counseling relationships have been discussed elsewhere (Bates & Johnson, 1969; Dreyfus, 1962). Our purpose in the following pages is to specify the implications of an existentialist stance for leaders of extensional groups.

The massive proliferation of "groups" today is a result of the alienation, loss of purpose, impersonalization, and dehumanization that all seem part of the *zeitgeist* of our times. If it is true that a particular philosophy reflects the *zeitgeist* of each age, the philosophy of existentialism most certainly reflects the anguish of mid-century humankind as we despair of "Truth" in a shattered world. The search for meaning, for encounter, for I-Thou, the confirmation of a universal *angst* as a basic condition, facing the loneliness of responsible choices — all these thread contemporary thought, and they have profound implications for the leader of an extensional group.

Many people perceive the existentialist philosophy as obscure and Godless, redundant and solipsistic, reactionary and anti-establishment. Others who have struggled with the convolutions of existentialist thought have found ideas that are lucid, spiritual, challenging, and comforting. Internalizing the concepts of this philosophy often has been, for those who persevere, an intense and personal experience. Group leaders who work from within an existentialist framework find that leading a group is an intense and personal experience.

The concepts of existentialism relevant to group processes are articulated below in the first person since they are highly personal statements. The implications for leaders of extensional groups are delineated next. Illustrative dialogues are provided where appropriate.

EXISTENTIALIST CONCEPT: EXISTENCE PRECEDES ESSENCE

A World Without Givens. I find myself thrown into a world void of all prior meaning. I find that I have arrived on the scene of life without a road map of the territory. I know one and only one certainty — death. Nothing else from this time on is a "given." No script has been written that I can consult. I am given no models, no "grand designs," no assurance that there is a teleological carpet that unfolds as I move toward death. I am on my own — alone.

I know that I exist. Now I must define myself and try to make meaning out of this world without meaning. I am completely free because there is no *a priori*. I am faced with the task of creating my world, which offers limitless possibilities without pre-established requirements. I exist. I find myself free to define my essence, and however I choose to define myself is up to me. I know that my statement concerning my essence will be unique, just as everyone's is unique. I know that I am different from any human being who ever lived before me or who ever will live after me, and I conceive of myself as fluid rather than static, moving rather than still, evolving rather than evolved, never finished.

My Signature of Essence. So I find that I am my own essence-giver. My life is an unanswered question to be answered however I choose. There are many times when I cry for the security of someone who will define me in the morass of this dreadful ambiguity, where all the certainty I have available is that at the end of my defining, death awaits. I know that I will be flung back into another unknown, perhaps like the unknown from which I was flung, but this time the unknown is ahead of me, an anticipation rather than a residual memory and — a certainty.

Between this terrible nothing and nothing I must make a statement concerning my essence. I am filled with *angst* because of the unknowns that dwell on either side of me. I cry for the security of "givens." I do not like being on my own, alone, undefined, forced to choose whatever I will. I feel a terrible nausea for life welling up in me. I would like to escape by default, to choose not to choose, but then this becomes a choice, and I meet myself face to face, filled with *angst* and despair.

26

My Primal and My Subsequent Choices. Out of my *angst* and nausea with life I must make a primal choice. I must choose to live or to die. Since for the moment I decide to live, I will live my life in such a way as to deserve something better than nothingness. I will use my becoming so as to deny the futility of existence and try to make my life a statement that ought never to be obliterated, even though I know that in the end it will be. Since essence is up to me, perhaps I can be worthy of existing and undeserving of being lost to the universe. I will try to have the courage to be. I will try to use my encounter with nothingness to affirm myself. I will try to have the courage to demonstrate my worth to a world in which my existence is not in question. I know that I exist, but I am aware that my *essence* is in question and I want my essence to be worthy of existing forever.

EXISTENCE PRECEDES ESSENCE: IMPLICATIONS FOR AN EXTENSIONAL GROUP

Group members as well as the leader are faced with the task of defining their essence. This concept is fundamental to the existential view of the nature of man. A group cannot define essence for its members, who all share the human state of being thrown from oblivion into an ambiguous world. It does not follow, however, that interaction is an empty ritual. At first glance, this would appear to be the case, for if each person must define himself or herself, what possible use could be made of group processes? If defining essence is an individual task, what place is there for the group relationship?

The answer lies in our essential loneliness. Each person is alone, but unaware of our essential state of isolation. If someone were dropped newborn on an unpopulated isle and by some miracle survived physically, that person would not become human in the existentialist sense. He or she could not define himself or herself without coming into contact with other humans. Only by interacting with another can a person become aware that he or she exists. Only through this interface can a person define self.

Group provides a rare and valuable opportunity to experience self through interacting with trained leaders and other members. Our need to define essence begs for opportunities to work with others, and a group experience can provide an unparalleled arena for this purpose. The essential, human lifelong task of defining essence is the most important process in which humankind will be involved, and it should not be left to casual relationships only. We exist. We must define our essence. Group is one place to record signatures and clarify existences.

In the conversation below the concept of human loneliness is being shared in a group:

> *Joan:* I feel uneasy when I walk into a room full of people. I don't know what to do, or say, or really, to be . . .

> *Lillie:* Yeah, that's how I am. I get tight inside, kind of queasy and don't know what to do, especially with my hands.

> *Joan:* Right now I'm experiencing the same feelings. Kind of tight, and sort of separate from you, and yet knowing you are here makes me feel stronger.

The Essence of the Group Leader

A group experience cannot change each member's essential sentence of having to define self, but it can midwife the process of becoming. Group members and leaders can walk together as each struggles with his or her essence. The group can share the pain of the constant metamorphosis that is becoming, and by sharing can be catalytic to the process. This sharing, however, holds special implications for the essence of the leaders. If leaders are destructive beings, a member can be hurt. If leaders are not authentic, a member can be hurt. If leaders are unskilled, a member can be hurt. The literature contains mounting evidence that counseling can be harmful. The naive and comforting assumption that at worst counseling may be ineffective is no longer tenable. Apparently, counselees who are counseled by counselors who are in poor psychological shape may leave the counseling relationship damaged (Carkhuff & Berenson, 1967). The profession's responsibility to ensure that this does not happen is obvious, as are the implications for selecting and training group leaders.

An example of a group leader being destructive might be:

Joan:	I've tried and tried to stand up to my boss, but I just can't do it. I just turn into a child every time he is around.
Destructive Leader:	You just have to be stronger. You aren't a little girl, you know, so why let him dominate you? Tell him off — tell him to go to hell — threaten to quit.

The existentialist concept of "existence precedes essence" involves counseling for leaders. Since a leader, too, is in the process of becoming, leaders need some source of what Carkhuff and Berenson have termed "human nourishment." The most elegant and harmonious choice for nourishment would be continuous, lifelong counseling — both individual and group — for the leader. Leading a group is stimulating, but demanding. Group leaders who are not members of groups may find themselves using the groups they lead for ther own needs, to the detriment of their group members. Who counsels the counselor is a relevant question for group leaders. Groups in which leaders can participate as members, where they can maintain their own growth toward self-actualization — "maintenance groups" for group leaders — seem essential as a way of professional life for those who lead groups.

Making Choices in an Extensional Group

The concept "existence precedes essence," with its reference to freedom, leaves us living an unanswered question. We must make choices and live by these choices. Since we must choose, our best chance of being human is to make as many choices as

29

possible in awareness. The existentialist struggles constantly to maintain this awareness of freedom by trying to view every word and every act as an active choice, and hence, an act of value creation.

One of the extensional group leader's tasks is to provide an atmosphere of safety so that each member may bring into awareness his or her own freedom, which involves making choices in no awareness, in dim awareness, or in full awareness. Participants through group processes can clarify the alternatives open to them and can increase their sensitivity toward aware choices. A group leader can help a member think through contradictions, ambiguities, value goals, and fantasies that may be action-inhibiting and that may have blocked growth.

A leader also can help members examine the consequences of alternatives. Members can be assisted to think through to logical conclusion various plans of action, and in so doing to become aware of freedom. Members also can examine the responsibility they carry for their chosen alternatives and face fully that they have no one on whom to shift this responsibility — neither counselor nor friend, teacher nor parent. They also must recognize that others will be affected by these actions and choices, and they must bring into awareness the effect of their choices on others, for this represents part of their individual responsibility.

Leaders must not overtly or covertly try to take away each member's responsibility in and out of group. Extensional group leaders are responsible for the group process, *not* for members. If a member chooses to be late, that is his or her choice; the leader begins on time. If a member chooses not to enter into the interaction, that is his or her choice; the leader creates the climate in which interaction is available.

A dialogue to illustrate the clarification of alternatives might be:

Jim: I can't get a job unless I cut my hair, but I think it looks creepy short . . .

Jane: You must not need a job very bad then.

Leader:	At the moment you seem pulled two ways . . .
Jim:	I really am. I do need the job.
Sue:	You could buy a wig and push your hair up under it when you go look for a job.
Jim:	If I don't have a job, I don't have any money to buy a wig, do I? Besides, I'd feel stupid in a wig. I suppose I could cut my hair some . . .
Leader:	Of the ideas, having your hair at least somewhat shorter seems one alternative to consider.

A dialogue to illustrate the responsibility for choices may be useful:

Harry:	I'm a listener. I want to be sure of what I say before I talk.
Al:	I think you're taking a free ride, Harry. You take from the group, but you don't give anything back.
Leader:	I relate to your choosing to talk on your own terms, Harry, but, Al, I also relate to your reaction. I feel like I'm not trustworthy with what you are about to share. I don't want to be the source of your need for certainty.

EXISTENTIALIST CONCEPT: HUMANKIND IS CONDEMNED TO FREEDOM

The Existentialist Paradox. I am free. No matter how much I would like to deny this awe-ful fact, I cannot. I am free — and this freedom contains a paradox. Because of my freedom, the pronoun "I" has absolute priority in my existence. I am the only one of my kind, and I cannot be classified. Since I am a singular phenomenon, I never will be repeated. I ought to be worthy of attention in the world. I can understand Morris' comment, "I am permanent, a datum written with indelible ink into the cosmic ledger book, never to be erased or expunged. I may be in very small print, but I am there forever. I assign to myself, therefore . . . an absolute value and an ultimate worth" (Morris, 1966, p. 16). Because I exist and I am I, the world would not be quite the same without me. This is one side of the existentialist paradox.

The other side of the paradox that I hold in awareness is that my existence is a great delusion, a huge joke, because, as I think of the magnitude of the universe, I know that I count for absolutely nothing. The universe is indifferent to my presence. When I die, there may be a moment of stirring, but then nothing. Sooner than later my absence will be forgotten, and eventually all traces of me will be erased from the universe. I try not to think of this inevitability too much because it brings on nausea and *angst*, but always I am haunted by awareness that my existence is completely irrelevant.

This is the paradox with which I live: to matter and not to matter, to be of absolute value in the world and to be of absolutely no value. These two truths are contradictory, but both are true. My subjectivity asserts the absoluteness of my value, and my reason asserts the veracity of my valuelessness. These two facts are paradoxical, but I believe them both as an inescapable result of my being condemned to freedom.

My Absolute Freedom: I Am My Values. The thought of my absolute freedom makes me angry. I do not wish to be free, to choose for myself, to be condemned to making choices on my own. Surely there is someone or something who will direct me and eliminate the boundlessness of my responsibility. As it is, I must stand witness for all my statements as to who I am. I have total personal answerability for my involvement in life.

It is dread indeed to be free and aware of my freedom. The responsibility for all my choices carries an added burden. As I make my choices, I create my value system. There is no one I can scapegoat, or blame, or burden with guilt. I would prefer an easier life, but I am free and am aware of my freedom. I am the sole author of my life, and I must answer for all I do. The statement that I make about myself is that I am ready to respond to each moment with authentic responsibility and am ready to speak for my performance.

This authenticity toward which I strive is illusive. I try to be honest inwardly and outwardly, but I am subject to error. At any given moment of being, I seem to myself to be authentic, but in backward glances I often find that my thoughts and behaviors were inconsistent with what I was really experiencing. I find that I cannot be wholly authentic, and this failure is a source of *angst* in me. I suffer pain because of anxiety and guilt generated by these failures. Intellectually I know that these failures are inevitable and a part of my human condition, but emotionally I react with a sense of incompleteness, a sense of never being total, a sense of freedom that is a burden rather than an inspiration.

There are rare moments when I transcend this sense of failure. At these times I am aware of moving forward, and I have a feeling of power over myself. In these instances I belong completely to myself and am in complete harmony with myself. I have the courage to be in full awareness, and I expect that in these moments I am truly authentic. At other times I can only use my sentence of freedom to strive toward authenticity and bear with what courage I can the *angst* that comes from failure. This is the inevitable tax levied with freedom, a price tagged to my condemnation.

HUMANKIND IS CONDEMNED TO FREEDOM: IMPLICATIONS FOR AN EXTENSIONAL GROUP

The Existentialist Paradox and Human Nourishment

The paradoxical nature of our freedom — to be of ultimate, absolute value and to be of absolutely no value — finds us in a condition of *angst* and nausea. We bring this *angst* and nausea to groups. The extensional group offers an antidote — human nourishment.

The concept of human nourishment applies especially to the extensional group. The notion that just as we need adequate physical nourishment daily in order to sustain good somatic health, so do we require daily human nourishment in order to sustain good psychological health, is particularly relevant to the idea of group as a vehicle for optimum personality development.

In a regressive, remedial group the concept of the group process functioning as a purgative or cathartic would be an apt parallel to the concept of human nourishment in an extensional group. One would hope that a remedial group would eventually begin to supply the basic minimum requirements of psychological food to its members until they would be able to develop to the point at which they could obtain it from their life-spaces outside the group. The extensional group provides this automatically as members seek to extend themselves in self-actualization. Human nourishment is a spinoff of the extensional group, but one that the leader can help members recognize as a basic need that may be sought actively in life outside the group. At present there seem to be no units for measuring the amounts of human nourishment taken in or given, although Berne's (1961) "strokes" might be one reference point.

It seems logical to assume that people who are in good psychological health themselves can give more human nourishment than can people who are operating at a lower level of functioning. The implications of this thought are profound for the group process. If, as Carkhuff and Berenson (1968) maintain, individual counseling can be "for better" or "for worse," a group almost certainly can be for better or for worse, too. Consequently, if someone is misplaced in a remedial group, the member may find that he or she gives nourishment but receives none in return, and upon leaving the group may feel badly diminished. In an extensional group the human nourishment available should be abundant so that no one need leave the group psychologically hungry.

A dialogue illustrating transmission of nourishment in a group follows:

Don:	I come to school in the morning and I just go to class day after day and I don't have any friends and I wonder what's wrong with me.
Cal:	I know what you mean. The only time I get to talk with anyone is lunch time or on the phone at night.
Leo:	I'm glad to know you both feel the way I do. I thought I was the only one who didn't seem to have friends and who was alone all the time.
Leader:	It seems to me that you are telling me that each of you is lonely and that you also feel better knowing that someone else is in the same boat — that there are others who feel the same way you do.

Existential Freedom and the Question of Values

The extensional group leader conceptualizes humankind as condemned to a freedom from which there is no escape. But the *degree* of awareness of that freedom differentiates existentialists from non-existentialists. The former, having become aware of the implications of their freedom, must stand up to it as best they can. The non-existentialist can enjoy the security of being other-directed.

At first glance the concept of freedom seems to pose problems for the extensional group leader, because the question of values is involved. Does the leader have the right to impose his or her values on a member?

Existentialism deals with this concern rather easily, for in this theoretical framework the question is irrelevant. Not only do leaders have no right to impose their values, but they *cannot* impose them, because each person is condemned to his or her own freedoms and must determine his or her own values. To raise the question of forcibly or subtly imposed values is to contradict the existentialist's concept of humankind as condemned to a freedom from which no escape is possible. This condition holds whether or not an individual is aware of his or her freedom; group leaders are condemned to freedom just as group members are.

The preceding notion in no way implies that leaders are not their value system. They are, and their values are transmitted full-force through their behaviors, but they do not and cannot impose these values on others. As leaders are available to members, so are their value systems available. Without this congruency, leaders could not be authentic. Leaders of extensional groups transmit to groups their feelings, their reactions, their essence. They are always aware, however, that their function as leaders is to midwife the growth of group members, not to use the group for the leader's own needs. As leaders of extensional groups interact with members, they are acutely aware that their sharing of authentic self is for the use of the group. Leaders are known, they are available, they are transparent, but they do not give advice or manipulate members. When they react and interact, they do so to extend the life-space of members. The fact that one's own life-space is expanded in the process is secondary to the primary purpose of being there — to be of use to the group.

An example of the dialogue that reflects translation of this concept into action might be:

Member (Cal):	I wish I could be honest with people, but they wouldn't understand if I told them the truth.
Leader (Joe):	I feel closed out without a chance to know if I *could* understand.

In this dialogue the leader is stating clearly his existent reactions — not for his needs (which might be to contradict, or be "better than," etc.) but to make his essence available to Cal, the member, who can use this content to hear what he really is saying: "I'm afraid I'll be rejected if I'm authentic; I prefer deceit," and so on.

EXISTENTIALIST CONCEPT:
ONE DEFINES SELF THROUGH ONE'S ACTIONS
AND ONLY THROUGH ONE'S ACTIONS

I am condemned by my human state to make free choices, and I know no reprieve from responsibility for those choices. On each choice I stake my future, and I am in a perpetual situation of crisis because I never am sure of the correctness of my choices. I also know that the way I define my essence is through my acts. I am continually emergent in my actions.

"What," Not "Why." I wish I could verbalize good intentions and get credit on the "books." I wish I could get credit for planning behavior and have it count, even though I didn't translate those plans into actions. But I know that my plans, my good intentions, my regrets, my *whys* are irrelevant until translated into action. Verbalizing a commitment to change is not action. What I actually do is my essence, my self-definition. Kierkegaard (1944) taught me this: that truth exists for a particular individual only as he or she produces it in action.

Thus, I must act before I count.

The "Here and Now." I do not restrict my conceptualization of action to overt acts but conceive my attitudes as part of the fabric of my actions. If I perform an act with reluctance, my reluctance defines some of that act. Everything that makes up my "I-ness" is relevant to my actions. The important idea of "I" is what I am *en toto*, and what I am now, this moment, here — not what I intend to be tomorrow, or what I intend to do tomorrow, or what I was yesterday, or what I did yesterday. This means that I must stand in present tense with complete accountability for what I am today, concerned about my past actions only as they are relevant for the present, and concerned about my future actions only as they are relevant for the present.

ONE DEFINES SELF THROUGH ONE'S ACTIONS: IMPLICATIONS FOR AN EXTENSIONAL GROUP

"Why" Versus "What" Counseling. Extensional group leaders who subscribe to the defining-through-action concept do not ask "Why?" of a group member; this is considered irrelevant. Rather, focus of group exploration is on "What." For example, a member coming to group with a conflict situation would not be faced with a futile cross-examination as to the causes of a behavior but would report the *what* of the circumstances. What were the behaviors and what does the member see as alternatives to this action? And since only the member is in charge of self and his or her actions, obviously any suggestion for solutions that requires a change of behavior by another person (e.g., a leader) would not be consistent with the concept of each person being responsible for defining oneself.

In a school extensional group, for instance, emphasis on the *what* behavior of a member permits the existentialist leader to avoid the pitfall of defending a colleague. Since focus is on actions of the participant, little attention is given to actions of a teacher or other persons concerned. This may distress a counselee who is accustomed to using a counselor as a sympathetic sounding board against whom to itemize the sins of others. The insistence of the existentialist counselor that the counselee talk about his or her own behaviors may at first be annoying, but as the counselee grows in self-respect and self-acceptance, the increasing awareness of responsibility will be refreshing.

Perhaps one of the reasons that counseling, both individual and group, is so often considered of little value by students is that group and individual sessions have been allowed to deteriorate into a self-pitying experience. The emphasis on *what* counseling, which is consistent with the concept of defining oneself through action, should prove far more productive to counselee and counselor alike.

Illustrative dialogue:

Mary: I try and try to be on time, but somehow I'm always late.

> *Leader:*   It seems to me that the thing you *do* is be late. The thing you *intend* to do is be on time.

The Here and Now. The existential concept of existence being in the here and now implies for the group leader that content is to focus mainly on the here-and-now process within the group. The fluid relating of one member to another provides the material of group exploration. As members react to each other, they are encouraged to verbalize this reaction. The current experiencing of each group member becomes the subject matter of each session. Concerns that each brings to the group are dealt with, of course, but the leader emphasizes existent reactions to those concerns and responds to the feelings of each member regarding the situation, rather than responding to the situation itself.

Dialogue in the here and now:

> *Diane:*   I'm really upset about what Joe did. He's mean and won't listen at all. He's impossible!

> *Leader:*   I'm receiving a lot of anger and frustration from you right now. I guess your statement about you is that you're pretty angry with Joe.

Each existent moment in group represents an existential moment when a member (and a leader) decides to define his or her essence with courage or decides passively to resign his or her humanity. The courage *to be* requires that one live in continuous confrontation in and out of group with one's being-in-the-world. A commitment to a decision-quality of human existence can be verbalized in the group. Living that commitment involves action outside the group.

Commitment stands on the statement: "This I am; this I believe; this I do. I am the being, the believing, the doing." Commitment is not a subscription to something external to one's life, but an awareness, an attitude, and a recognition of the feeling of being fully present in a moment, making choices in that moment, and standing on the consequences of those choices. Participation in life and in the group is a consequence of genuine commitedness to living in which one freely chooses one's being in action. If a person takes responsibility for his or her life and expresses it through participation, he or she is totally involved, totally committed (Bugenthal, 1965). A participant can practice participative behavior in group life and perhaps increase involvement and commitment in life outside the group. The extensional group is an arena in which commitments can be articulated and extended into a member's entire life-space.

EXISTENTIALIST CONCEPT: THE ENCOUNTER — THE "I - THOU" RELATIONSHIP DEFINES GROUP PROCESSES AND CONTENT

When I think of the "I-Thou" relationship, I become uneasy at times. What I must do to create this relationship is to communicate somehow my essence —open, uncensored, vulnerable. I do not always want to do this, partly because it will be, as it must be, only a shadow of my "I-ness," and also because in reaching I-to-thou I am risking the pain of being misunderstood or unaccepted. I would rather be safe in my obscurity. I would like to hide behind an anonymous mask; then no other could encounter the "I" of me, nor I, the "Thou" of the other. Thus, we never meet — and hurt. But also, we never meet — and love.

Journey into Life-Space. So I seek out the encounter "I-to-Thou," for here is where I exercise my being. In the encounter we live each other, reciprocating uniqueness and singularity. I enter the arena of another's life-space, vulnerable to all that is there. I am not neutral, but am involved and committed. I risk pain and error, but I do this in awareness that encounter confirms my humanness, my authenticity, and my essence, just as it confirms the humanity, authenticity, and essence of Thou — all humankind. As I comprehend the essence of another, I take him or her into myself and allow myself to be taken into him or her, throwing open the gates of my being. We both experience an increasing inner richness.

This journey into the life-space of Thou is not easy for me. I must lower my defenses, allow my shields to go down, and, in a curious fashion, turn myself off, partially losing awareness of myself as a being with needs, drives, and perceptions as I try to enter the awareness of another. I do not know exactly how I do this, except that the act, I know, requires deep concentration, intense involvement, and maximum energy on my part.

In and out of encounter, I strive for perfect authenticity, but never am I complete, so I never outwardly transmit exactly what I am inwardly. I am

39

never wholly congruent, but I struggle constantly toward becoming, always in the process of self-actualizing, never self-actualized. This imperfection becomes a source of *angst*, of anxiety, to me. I would like to be completed, but I cannot attain total authenticity, which I know is as unattainable as total encounter.

THE ENCOUNTER: IMPLICATIONS FOR THE EXTENSIONAL GROUP

In the I-Thou relationship, the group leader enters a member's life-space and shares what he or she sees there. In openness and mutuality the existentialist leader allows the worlds of the participants to unfold during an encounter. This requires that the leaders actively attempt to enter the members' worlds — not simply listen to them passively. The climate of the group is generated from empathy, congruency, and specificity on the leader's part. Members are helped to experience existence as real, to increase their abilities to extend potentialities and expand alternatives. Group members are assisted through the group process to affix their signatures to their own statement of essence.

The extensional leader views members of the group as unique, dynamic individuals, not as statistical norms. Each member is not an object to whom things are done, but a subject with whom action possibilities are explored. Each participant is treated with dignitiy as a *person*, whether child, adolescent, or adult. The leader encounters the person, regardless of age, as a being of ultimate value — a person who, like the leader, is engaged in defining essence out of ambiguous freedom.

Journey into Life-Space. Lewin's (1935) conceptualization of each individual existing in a life-space with parameters defined by the boundary that exists between self and the environment has application to the group process and relevancy to the existential concept of *encounter.* A person's life-space is dynamically a relatively closed system that attempts to maintain equilibrium under the impact of field forces, negative and positive valences. The various life-spheres (profession, family, friendships with definite persons, etc.), as well as different needs, become more and more differentiated as a person expands his or her life-space and extends psychical regions and systems within that life-space.

Encounter involves explorations of an individual's life-space. As one group member describes the territory of her psychical sphere, other members and leaders "track" her verbalizations and in the process help the member understand, appreciate, and identify the forces in her idiosyncratic field. In a somewhat mystical sense the experience of a group focusing on the life-space of one member illuminates that space with the group's energies. As group members journey into the life-spaces of others in the group, human nourishment is given and received; insight concerning the realities of each individual's life-space also is gained. Somehow, as group members and leaders "walk around" in one another's existences, obscured blocks to growth are identified and may then be dealt with. Characteristic life-styles can be identified, too. A dialogue of such a journey is used for illustration.

> *Harriet:*   I look around my world and it's all colored blue, and the people in it have dim faces. They aren't sad, but they aren't happy either.
>
> *Leader:*   The way you describe it, they don't have much form, just seem to be blurs.
>
> *Harriet:*   Yeah, people really don't have much meaning for me. Sometimes I think I just use them to get out of them what I want but don't see a real person behind the faces.
>
> *Leader:*   Like right now, for instance, you seem somehow cut off, kind of in the distance, not quite right here, and I'm wishing I could reach you.

In addition to illuminating the life-space of each individual group member, the group process can be used to explore the relationship of one member's life-space to another's. The group leader must function actively during this experience. A leader's responsibility is to aid members to encounter one another, and to do this he or she must keep channels of communication open. The leader must insist that members make clear the hypotheses they might attempt to hide through using an interrogation approach. The leader must refuse to allow one member to "hook" another on a question, but must insist that the questioner make a statement about where he or she stands.

In adhering to this concept, the leader constantly emphasizes that each member is speaking only for himself or herself. The leader encourages frequent use of "I's" on the part of group members. He or she insists that members talk face-to-face, never about another. The leader calls attention to members' reliance on the "they" world for legitimizing their personal stances and insists that each make his or her individual position clear. The leader translates generalities into concrete specifics.

The existential emphasis on being self-responsible and appreciating the importance of acting and being in the here and now is comparable with gestalt counseling procedures and techniques. The later chapters on leader functions discuss several techniques and group procedures taken from gestalt psychology (Passons, 1975).

To contrast the existential model with others, Appendix A at the end of this book gives historical foundations for five models, including the existential. A bibliography for further reference is included.

SUMMARY

The preceding pages have identified some concepts of existentialism that are relevant to the extensional group. The philosophy has been presented from a personal point of view, then translated into implications for the extensional group process. Illustrative dialogues have been included.

REFERENCES

Bates, Marilyn, and Johnson, C. D. "The Existentialist Counselor at Work," *School Counselor*, March 1969, pp. 245-50.

Berne, Eric. *Transactional Analysis*. New York: Grove Press, 1961.

Bugenthal, J. F. T. *The Search for Authenticity*. New York: Holt, Rinehart, and Winston, 1965.

Carkhuff, Robert R., and Berenson, Bernard C. *Counseling and Therapy*. New York: Holt, Rinehart, and Winston, 1967.

Dreyfus, Edward A. "Counseling and Existentialism," *Journal of Counseling Psychology*, Vol. 9, No. 2, 1962, pp. 128-34.

Kierkegaard, Soren. *The Concepts of Dread*. Princeton, NJ: Princeton University Press, 1944. (translated by Walter Lowrie)

Lewin, Kurt. *A Dynamic Theory of Personality*. New York: McGraw-Hill, 1935.

Morris, Van Cleve. *Existentialism in Education*. New York: Harper and Row, 1966.

Passons, William R. *Gestalt Approaches in Counseling*. New York: Holt, Rinehart, and Winston, 1975.

3

Conceptual Frameworks for Understanding Individual Behavior in the Group

- Jungian Typology
    - Analytical and Feeling Types
    - Intuitive and Sensate Types
    - Extrovert and Introvert Types
    - Structure and Flow Types
    - Conclusion

- FIRO (Fundamental Interpersonal Relationship Orientation)
    - Inclusion
    - Control
    - Affection
    - Conclusion

- The Johari Window
    - Cell I: Area of Free Activity
    - Known to Me — Known to You

    - Cell IV: Area of the Unknown
    - Unknown to Me — Unknown to You

    - Cell III: Private Life-Space Area
    - Known to Me — Unknown to You

    - Cell II: Risk Area, The Group Arena
    - Unknown to Me — Known to You

    - Conclusion

- Summary

3

Conceptual Frameworks for Understanding Individual Behavior in the Group

The thought of control is repugnant to most group leaders, and the suggestion of manipulation is equally distasteful. Thus, when the recommendation is made that group leaders, through their facilitative functions, both control and manipulate group processes, the initial reaction may be one of horror. Yet, that is exactly what group leaders do — control and manipulate the *processes* of group interaction. They never, under any circumstances, attempt to control and manipulate the participants. To control the group processes, however, the leader needs conceptual frameworks from which to understand the participants' interactive behaviors that make up the group processes. These frameworks are in addition to the theoretical frameworks in Chapter 1, which described levels of self-disclosure and the model from which extensional group leaders operate.

We will consider three conceptual frameworks: (1) Jungian typologies (Jung, 1923; von Franz & Hillman, 1975; Kiersey & Bates, 1978), (2) FIRO — Fundamental Interpersonal Relationship Orientation (Schutz, 1966, 1971, 1973), and (3) the Johari Window (Luft & Ingram, 1963; Luft, 1969). The sequence of the three concepts is intended first to attend to how people *can* differ substantially (Jung's typologies) in the way they interpret and make sense out of their environments. Second, all people have interpersonal needs (FIRO), but they do not all have them to the same extent. Expecting all group members to have the same degree of interpersonal need for interaction would be naive, or, for some group leaders, insensitive. Third, after gaining an appreciation for individual differences in perceptions and needs, a group leader's efforts can be guided toward productive interaction if he or she has a cognitive structure (Johari Window) for observing *how* people interact. Some types of interaction are less helpful than others as the extensional model is applied.

JUNGIAN TYPOLOGY

Carl Jung hypothesized that there are at least four distinct ways of viewing and interpreting information and data available to us from our environment. The four psychological styles of viewing our experiences are: analytical, feeling, intuitive, and sensate (the senses — seeing, hearing, etc.). Each of us possesses all four styles at the same time, but each of us prefers one type to the others.

For example, imagine four persons attending a play. One person enjoys analyzing the interrelationships of the characters, the story line, and the intricacies of the play. His companion may assess the play according to the affect she experiences. Viewing a play makes her feel good or bad, excited or bored, and so on. Another viewer in the foursome may have taken a look at the program before curtain time, immediately summed up in his mind what the play was about, who the interesting characters would be, and what the play's outcome would be. The fourth playgoer may be fascinated by the staging, lighting, costumes, and clarity of the lines. Her appreciation centers on how well the details of the play are put together.

Having a basic understanding of typologies alerts group leaders to possible interferences in interpersonal communication as people interact. When we talk with those whose preferred style matches our own, they seem readily comprehensible. On the other hand, if we are interacting with someone whose style or type is the opposite of our own, we may have somewhat different versions of reality, even though we are discussing the same thing. Because we are both looking at the same reality, but through different lenses, so to speak, we will probably arrive at different conclusions and interpretations. The tendency then is to think of the other person as stupid or deceitful. Having a fundamental awareness, understanding, and appreciation that differences in perceptions exist *naturally* is helpful to leaders in maintaining their objectivity and openness.

Because the authors wish to present only enough discussion to make the reader aware of typologies, our description will be simple and relatively brief. A thorough discussion of this fascinating area of human differences is beyond the scope of this book. For a more comprehensive and intelligent review of Jungian typology, we refer the reader to the three books cited earlier in this chapter. But let's look at the different types in relation to the concept of Jungian typologies.

Analytical and Feeling Types

An analytical person would look at the concept of Jungian typology in terms of how the system fits together. What are the causes and effects? What variables must be examined to comprehend the system of psychological types? Being cognitive and cerebral is most important to analytical individuals' satisfaction when they consider their experience. Relatively little *affect* (but a lot of *effect*) is involved when an analytical person is trying to make sense out of his or her world. When interacting with analytical "types," the leader must remember to concentrate on the reasoning processes in which these people prefer to engage.

In contrast to analytically oriented people are those who prefer to process the meaning of their experiences according to feelings they recognize within themselves. Feeling people tend to make decisions and judgments in terms of the kind of affect triggered by a situation. Feeling people understand the concept of Jungian typology, for example, primarily by whether they like it or not. If they feel good about the concept, it has merit. Feeling people look at their world through affective glasses. When observing and interacting with a feeling-type person, a group leader must remember to concentrate on the emotions that might arise for this member.

Analyzing and feeling types are considered opposites. The more analytical a person is, the less affective he or she is likely to be, and vice versa. Analyzing and feeling types who understand their differentness often interact beneficially, because one gives clarity to a problem or issue while the other provides the motives for action.

Intuitive and Sensate Types

An intuitive type of person characteristically trusts hunches. He or she is an instinctive individual, often unaware as to *how* the hunch came about. That isn't important to intuitive people anyway, because details typically are unimportant to them. Intuitives are quick to grasp the total picture of a problem or issue but do not necessarily know how to do something about it at the moment. Intuitive persons form opinions of the Jungian typology concept in a flash. They can foresee how the concept might be useful and are stimulated to speculation that probably has no connection with anything occurring in the here and now. We must remember that symbolisms and global kinds of attention are preferred when interacting with group members who are primarily intuitive.

Sensate people are alert to information acquired through the senses (e.g., seeing, hearing, touch). They prefer fine detail and are normally content with routine activities that are attended to in the here and now. Sensates are "finishers" in that they enjoy closure. A sentence with a period, a story with a conclusion, is far more satisfactory to them than is the mystery of open-endedness. Sensates can be attracted to Jungian typology if they can actually see and hear people behaving according to the types. Group leaders, when interacting with a sensate, should focus on concrete experience and facts.

Although intuitives and sensates are considered opposites, they can be great working partners when they acknowledge and appreciate each other's uniqueness. A sensate, for example, remembers intricate details in a novel, while the intuitive quickly comprehends the entire plot but might not remember the name of the the hero! When working together, an intuitive person offers a creative vision of what *can* be done while the sensate person does the "pick-and-shovel" work necessary to achieve the vision.

Extrovert and Introvert Types

As we have seen, people may be analytical, feeling, intuitive, and sensate types. They also differ in the extent to which they wish to include others in their processing of experience. This continuum is bordered by *extroverts* and *introverts*. An extroverted person wants a lot of people involved to provide input as part of making sense out of living. An introverted person has an opposite need — solitude. Introverts are satisfied about processing their reality information inside themselves. They do not depend upon information or input from others.

To illustrate how personality variables or types might be combined, think of how an extroverted, analytically oriented person views his or her reality. This person prefers to study his or her world *with* other people to share ideas and interests. An introverted, analytically oriented person would rather study his or her world alone.

Structure and Flow Types

One other dimension in terms of the way we process information and relate to our world focuses on our preference to have information in a structured, predictable form or to accept and deal with information as it comes, whenever and wherever crisis or delight hits us. These two extremes in processing information are referred to as *structure* and *flow*. People who prefer structure and are also analytically oriented probably do their best work at their desks at regular times. Flow, analytically oriented people may just as easily figure things out while taking a shower, at a ball game, or in the middle of the night when they cannot sleep.

Each of us has a combination of personality factors that, when summed up, become our frame of reference. There are numerous combinations, but addressing all possible variations and combinations is beyond the scope of this discussion. The main point is that the leader should learn to recognize communication that is insensitive to unique frames of reference (types), for such interaction is unproductive to the group process. Although the following is not an illustration from group, examining the kind of interaction that can take place between individuals of unlike typology may be helpful in understanding how a lack of awareness between interacting people can diminish a relationship.

A married couple seeking counseling opened their first session with, "We have nothing in common anymore. We can't even talk to each other." As they revealed their problems, it became apparent that they were probably looking at their marriage relationship through distinctly different frames of reference, though neither mate had considered this possibility. Something was "wrong" with a mate who simply "refused to understand or cooperate."

A Jungian typology assessment inventory was administered (Yabroff, 1978), and the results confirmed their uniqueness. They were opposite psychological types. The husband was extroverted and highly structured. He was keenly analytical and preferred trusting his senses. He was an engineer who liked his world best when it was predictable. His wife was a shy, spontaneous person who was emotional and believed in extrasensory perception. She attended art classes regularly and enjoyed them as an outstandingly creative student. She was not concerned about her generally unplanned days or serving dinner at 5:30 or 6:00 p.m. Until the last minute she did not even think about what the menu would be.

The couple's interaction was punctuated with frequent bickering. Because the wife processed her experiences through feelings, she often asked her husband how he "felt" about something. But feelings did not compute in his analytical style of processing. She then became irritated at what she thought to be his lack of concern. He continually asked her for facts to support her decisions, when in her mind a hunch was a sufficient basis for making decisions like buying a new refrigerator. He was exasperated at her sloppy attention to the checkbook, while his meticulous care for detail drove her "up the wall."

A pending vacation was the culminating event that prompted them to seek counseling. He wanted every day of their vacation planned — where they were going to stay, what they were going to do, how much money they should take, and so on. She argued for getting in the car and "wandering where the spirit takes us," because schedules and lists hampered her enjoyment. The arguing became bitter, loud accusations were uttered, old hostilities were uncorked and unloaded. The wife dissolved into tears in the locked bedroom, foreseeing the possible demise of their relationship. The husband went to his favorite bar to figure things out with the help of his drinking friends.

Resolution of their interpersonal conflict could not begin until they learned to accept and appreciate the distinctive nature of each other's frame of reference.

Conclusion

Having a basic understanding of the typology concept can help the leader influence improved communication between group members. Arguments and debates are often signals that individuals of differing types are each attempting to validate *their own* reality and experiences. When something so clear (to me) is not being comprehended or accepted by another person, only two explanations are possible: The other person is either "not too bright" or "trying to pull a fast one." Without a group leader's guidance, endless discussion focusing on who is "right" and who is "wrong" can absorb inordinate amounts of time to no productive end.

A leader's attitude of acceptance and appreciation for varying frames of reference serves as a model for group members.

The leader can also short-circuit dialogue that appears to be futilely attempting to prove one member's "rightness" against another member's "wrongness." Formal training in techniques and strategies designed specifically to overcome individual differences may be helpful, but it is not absolutely necessary. Simply being aware of differing frames of reference and recognizing the naturalness of unique differences helps a leader remain objective and certainly aids a leader's effectiveness. This is particularly true during times when group members are having difficulty understanding each other's frames of reference.

Confusion, disagreement, and negative feelings are not automatically discouraged in extensional groups, because they can be explored and, it is hoped, rechanneled constructively. The group leader, however, must have some idea as to the source of those feelings in an individual in order to implement strategies that will influence the group's positive interactive process.

Instruments for assessing psychological types have been devised (Myers, 1962; Kiersey & Bates, 1978; Yabroff, 1978). We believe that they have value primarily as instructional aids and as discussion stimulators. As clinical tools, their value is limited.

FIRO (FUNDAMENTAL INTERPERSONAL RELATIONSHIP ORIENTATION)

Having considered how psychological types filter and contribute to *intra*personal meaning, we can begin to appreciate that each human being is a unique combination of experiences, expectations, capabilities, values, motives, and belief systems. Interestingly, the appreciation for uniqueness is easiest when we are talking *about* it rather than dealing *with* it. Observing unique human beings in action can be baffling sometimes, especially when trying to comprehend the *inter*personal dynamics between group participants. Why do some group members hold back while others are almost compulsive about getting to know everyone? How is it that some people simply ooze warmth and caring while others recoil at the possibility of being touched? Why do some group members continually argue with the group leader and others seemingly refuse to take any form of responsibility for the group? Having a conceptual framework for organizing and making sense of what is happening between group members can be helpful in a group leader's decision-making about how to proceed. Futhermore, when one begins to witness the *many* patterns of interaction, appreciation of human uniqueness acquires substance and practical meaning.

William Schutz (1958, 1971, 1973) has described three basic interpersonal needs — *inclusion, control,* and *affection. Each of these three interpersonal needs can be viewed in terms of the way we express our needs to others and the way we want others to meet our needs.*

Inclusion

Imagine entering a room of relative strangers, say, at a social gathering. Some people immediately begin saying "hello," start conversations, and appear totally comfortable with initiating the process of getting acquainted with others. They are *including* themselves in the gathering. Other people do not initiate contact, preferring to sit back and wait for others to approach them. There is a degree to which we want others to make the effort to include us in the gathering. Some shy people, for example, do nothing to initiate contact with others, but they welcome the overtures of others. Then, some people do not care one way or the other whether people notice them or attempt to include them.

When a person is labeled "stuck up," the implication is that the person is arrogant and aloof. One should temper hasty conclusions in this regard, however. We all have varying needs for inclusion (the extent to which we want to be noticed by others). Some people have low need, which has nothing to do with their judgment of others, but means that they simply do not need a lot of attention. Conceivably, a person may have a high need to initiate interpersonal contact (a "glad-hander" perhaps) and not care whether or not others want him or her. On the other hand, a "wallflower" does nothing to initiate interpersonal contact but desperately hopes to be invited to dance. Usually the two aspects of inclusion are relatively balanced — i.e., gregarious people usually hope for a receptive audience, and people who tend to hold back from making contact are likely to be selective about which outsiders, and how many of them, are permitted into their private worlds.

The authors have sometimes used a group exercise (1) to help participants understand the inclusion concept experientially and (2) to gain a clue as to members' inclusion needs. The room is cleared of obstructions. The group is instructed to stand and form a tight circle. One member is randomly designated to drop out and attempt to re-enter the group, which is instructed to prevent re-entry. The drop-out is told to use any method he or she chooses — cajoling, reasoning, persuading, tickling, force, etc., to re-enter the group. In addition to some uproarious fun and laughter, profound insights may come from the experience. The group members begin to explore their attitudes about rejecting someone and to contrast their pity for the excluded person with their loyalty to the group's "mission" of exclusion.

One one occasion a hulking male group member felt so sorry for a petite female drop-out that he opened his part of the circle to let her in. The group expressed their unhappiness with him in no uncertain terms. What authority had he to make a decision that should have been made by the entire group? On another occasion a drop-out discovered something in his style of interpersonal interaction that astounded him. Instead of making any effort to re-enter the circle, he simply sat down. Soon the group began to encourage him, eventually begging him to rejoin the main body. Later, during discussion, he expressed his shock at discovering his customary interpersonal style in real-life situations. Although he acknowledged his own need to be part of a social milieu, he did little to initiate contact with others. Instead, he was inclined to wait for others to come to him and then judged them negatively if they did not.

In later chapters we will be examining techniques for facilitating group process. If the reader has comprehended Schutz's idea of *inclusion* needs, it should be easy to appreciate that quiet group members are not necessarily resistive. A leader who understands the idea of inclusion and has a hunch about members' inclusion needs can begin to adapt his or her efforts with a sensitivity to each member's unique needs for inclusion.

Control

Schutz makes an interesting comparison between inclusion needs and control needs. Inclusion, he has written, is a matter of predominance, whereas control is a matter of dominance. A person who has a high need for interpersonal control likes being in charge, to make decisions for and about others, and to be a significant influence in what happens. A person with a low need for interpersonal control prefers that others be responsible for themselves. We also must consider the degree to which we like others to control us. A highly dependent person needs to have others making decisions, and, conversely, an independent person resists being controlled. In arguments or differences of opinion high controllers want to *win*, and they resist perceived authority. Low controllers generally have a "live and let live" attitude. They are not even particularly concerned about the issue of control. It is possible for one person to have almost opposite control needs; e.g., an army sergeant may enjoy barking orders at recruits (high need to control others) and eagerly comply with orders from the commander (high need to *be* controlled by others). For the most part, however, there is usually an inverse correlation in control needs; the person who wants to be the boss normally does not like to take orders from others.

Here is a group exercise that focuses on the control need issue. It is always fun and usually provides insights into an individual's attitude about control. Members of the group are instructed to line up, shoulder to shoulder, according to their self-image as controllers. High controllers are to position themselves at one end of the line and low controllers at the other. The line must remain shoulder to shoulder, although participants are free to reposition themselves if they think their relative position in line does not represent their attitude about control.

If one person is standing in the position desired by another participant, a lively debate and sometimes shoving and jostling ensue as two or more participants vie for the same "uncontrolling" position. Usually, a few participants drift about aimlessly, not particularly caring where their position is because they care nothing about controlling or being controlled. Other individuals intentionally go to the high-control end of the line, because they perceive themselves as high controllers and are not ashamed to be so identified.

Specific techniques and suggestions as to how to deal with high and low controllers are presented in Chapter 7. Group participants who are high controllers do not necessarily mean "trouble" for a group leader. Low controllers can cause more concern to a leader because of their unwillingness to be responsible or take a stand. At this point we simply wish to point out that apparently resistive or belligerent group members (high controllers) are displaying only a part of their interpersonal needs. Likewise, group members who are dependent, wanting others to decide and take responsibility, are revealing only a part of their interpersonal needs.

Affection

The third interpersonal need area is *affection*, which is loosely defined as warmth and caring. It characterizes the way an individual feels toward others and the way the individual wants others to feel toward him or her. Schutz, in defining affection, includes a wide range of positive feelings. We can have a good feeling about someone we have just met, and we can have passionate feelings about an intimate. The focus is the extent to which we express our feelings toward others. Are we generous in hugging, stroking (verbally and physically), and expressing our positive feelings for others? Moreover, consider our degree of willingness to have others express their feelings toward us. A person who has low affection needs is not necessarily hateful. He or she simply may not have the same needs as a person who wants affection from others and enjoys expressing it as well.

A revealing group exercise concerning affection is called the "mill-in." Members of the group are instructed to roam about the room to locate a spot that suits them. As they roam, they are free to express their feelings toward group mates in any non-verbal fashion they choose. Handshakes, pats on the back, smiles, hugs, and sometimes kisses are shared. Inevitably, several participants actively avoid making contact and "roam" in an opposite direction from "huggers." Schutz's concept of affection is vivid in this exercise. Some people assert their affectionate feelings, while others deal with these feelings in an entirely different manner. For some it is easier to initiate expressions of affection than to receive expressions of affection. Others are reluctant to display affection but are delighted to have others display affection toward them. And some individuals truly care nothing about affection displays.

Conclusion

As a group leader develops sophistication, it becomes possible to observe the group's interaction move through the three interpersonal need areas. In the opening session, if the members are strangers, inclusion needs prevail. The participants are wondering, "Who are these people, and how will I relate to them?" "Do I want to become involved with these people?" Once the inclusion issue is resolved, individual members begin jockeying for power in the form of wanting to be perceived as competent and influential. "Which group members seem to be the wisest, most compassionate, and alert?" "Which members are the better/best participants?" "Is anyone taking the leader to task?"

Bidding for power, influence, and dominance can be subtle, but it *will* be present. It has been said that if, for some reason, a group of strangers were to be assembled, a leader would naturally emerge. Leadership is a form of control (power), and the designated leader must be aware of his or her own style of leadership, as well as sensitive to the control needs of group participants.

After the inclusion and control needs are clarified, affection is the next stage of group development in an extensional group.

Openness, trust, and warmth are shared by group members who have consciously (or unconsciously) come to terms with their inclusion and control needs. They are comfortable with their identity in the group and have assessed the potential importance of their contribution to the group. Group members who view themselves as misfits may never resolve their need for being competent. People perceived as incompetent are difficult to love, and their attempts at being warm and caring are not easily accepted.

Although the complexity of the various interpersonal need patterns can be overwhelming, awareness of the three interpersonal needs provides a basic conceptual framework for organizing experience and observation. Adroitneses at altering strategies and techniques is an art rather than a skill, but the leader needs a beginning framework nonetheless. Being aware of the three interpersonal needs is a foundation. Group members *do* indeed vary in their uniqueness. They have their own needs and their own contributions to make to the group. This statement is more than a platitude; it is a practical fact that cannot be ignored. The FIRO concept is one way of organizing the interactive needs of group participants.

Schutz has developed a respected instrument for assessing interpersonal needs (Schutz, 1977), but, as in the Jungian typologies, the authors value it only as an instructional device for teaching and understanding the FIRO concepts.

THE JOHARI WINDOW

The Johari Window offers the group leader and members a framework that provides direction for the group processes. The exotic title for the Window comes from a combination of the first names of the two men who put the original model together — Joseph Luft and Harry Ingham — hence, Joe-Hari. The original model delineated the relationship of one person (represented by four cells) to others. The following adaptation of Luft and Ingham's conceptual scheme is suggested as a means of ordering the group processes and content into a simple cognitive map that provides direction for both leaders and members.

We suggest that group leaders present the general idea of the Window, as outlined here, in an orientation session, to give potential participants a road map of the group process, as well as an understanding of their responsibilties as group members. At this point leaders, too, through the Window, are clarifying the safeguards to privacy that they will provide to participants. Figure 3.1 is an adaptation of the Johari Window to the extensional group model. The following comments on the application of the Window to this group model are presented in the order suggested for the orientation session.

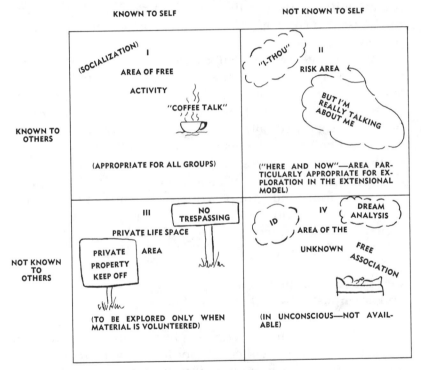

FIGURE 3.1
A Cognitive Map of Group Processes
(Adapted for Groups from the Johari Window)

Originally formulated by Joseph Luft and Harry Ingham in "The Johari Window, A Graphic Model of Awareness in Interpersonal Relations," in *Group Processes: An Introduction to Group Dynamics* by Joseph Luft (Palo Alto: National Press Books, 1963), pp. 10-12.

Cell I: Area of Free Activity
Known to Me — Known to You

The first cell of the Window represents content that is known to me about me and is readily available or is known to others. This content is the fabric of social intercourse around which we build our daily interchanges (e.g., we all know that the writers of this book are interested in groups; we all know that we write; and so forth). Out of this knowledge, known to me about me and known to you about me, can be built a commonality of interest that may lead to friendship. We routinely use this content area in social situations to build and to perpetuate relationships.

We operate in this cell as we interface daily with one another. As we expand the size of Cell I, we come to know more and more about each other, and we may come to care more and more for each other. The content material of this cell is primarily cognitive, although it may contain some conative content. The prime characteristic of the content is that it is typical of material we deal with in routine activities. Therefore, though it is useful as a vehicle from which to build group communication and group acquaintanceship, interaction in this cell is *not* unique to a group, but may be obtained in a variety of circumstances.

Cell IV: Area of the Unknown
Unknown to Me — Unknown to You

Cell IV represents material that by definition is unavailable — the unconscious. Neither you nor I know what resides in my unconscious. It may be brought into awareness through hypnosis, or free association, or dream analysis, but without special efforts it remains below the level of awareness. Exploration of this cell in the usual interaction group is not appropriate. For the leader to deal with these kinds of materials requires a high degree of skill and training; thus the cell is "off limits" for extensional groups.

Cell III: Private Life-Space Area
Known to Me — Unknown to You

Cell III represents the area that is most often violated in the name of group process. Destructive group experiences usually center in this cell. Travesties mislabeled "group encounters" and "sensitivity groups" center in this cell. If groups are perceived as a negative force, it is probably because the perceiver conceptualizes groups as operating from this cell. The leader and members maybe probed into the private life-spaces represented by this cell, and violated human dignity.

This cell represents the body of knowledge each of us knows about ourselves but which we do not know about anyone else. This knowledge concerns our private, personal lives. If, in a group, members or leader intrude into that private, personal area, they have trespassed into another's life-space. No one in a group is welcomed to solicit through questioning or any other means material from Cell III. When members *volunteer* content from their private, personal life-space, then and only then is it available to the group. Until that time, the "No Trespassing" sign must be observed.

Group leaders must protect the Cell III area of each member; the traffic-directing function (Chapter 5) helps leaders achieve this end. Wise leaders do not allow members to probe into private areas of one another's lives. They do not allow one member to volunteer another member's Cell III material. They are constantly alert to make sure that no one does so, nor do leaders do so themselves. They make it clear that members may say, "I do not wish to discuss that," without being labeled "bad group members" or being accused of having a "hangup" about something. Astute leaders recognize that Cell III is where "groupies" practice their merry games, all in the name of an "honesty" that could be more accurately described as "psychological infiltration."

A group member may choose to bring concerns from Cell III of his or her life-space to the group, where they can be discussed. The material, however, must directly concern that person and not others close to him or her. Participants in interaction groups sometimes inappropriately introduce material that concerns the Cell III life-space of significant others in their lives. Consider, for example, a member who relates that his wife is a sloppy housekeeper and cannot manage their money. The alert group leader immediately realizes that the member is intruding into the Cell III life-space of his wife, and suggests that the group member deal with *his* feelings about the situation, not his wife's behaviors. The focus thus is maintained on the existent experience in the here and now of the group member, not on the past or present experience in the there and then — in this instance, a wife's housekeeping behaviors.

In regard to Cell III material, the issue of confidentiality usually arises. In some groups, members are requested to keep confidential all material discussed in the group; the content at issue would be derived from this cell. Although a group leader certainly does not want to discourage members from exploring concerns they have from their own Cell III, he or she does take the risk of confidentiality being violated each time material from this area is introduced.

When students are involved, material from Cell III must be handled with particular care because the school group leader has no way of guaranteeing confidentiality on behalf of student group members. Thus, his or her only recourse is to strongly discourage exploration of material from Cell III that would violate the privacy of a member's family. If a student wishes to discuss a family argument, the leader should block content description and assist the member in dealing with here and now feelings and behaviors in the group; then, if necessary, the leader can see the student privately.

Cell II: Risk Area, The Group Arena
Unknown to Me — Known to You

If a leader takes the position that Cell I is useful — but *not* unique — to groups and is available in a variety of settings, that Cell IV is by definition not available, that Cell III invades privacy and may be volunteered only if it concerns oneself, what areas can be tapped so that the group process is productive? The answer lies in Cell II. Here can be found material unique to groups and, in usual human interface, not tapped.

There is a body of material that is known to *you* about me but that *I* do not know about me, that is known to *me* about you but that *you* do not know about you. This risk area concerns the way I am experiencing you and the way you are experiencing me. You, and *only* you, are the sole source of information about how you are reacting to me, and I have no way of obtaining these data until you are willing to give them to me. Conversely, I, and only I, am the sole source of information about how I am reacting to you, and you have no way of obtaining these data until I give them to you.

If the uniqueness of the group process is to be tapped, I must be willing to give you feedback out of this risk area. As I communicate with you concerning my responses to you, it must be understood that there will be no implication that you should change. You may or may not choose to do so. If a number of group members experience the same reaction, you may give the feedback more weight; on the other hand, you may choose only to recognize their statements as useful information to be "filed."

Cell II taps solely the *here and now* of the group process — how one member is experiencing another in that existent moment. Content does not deal with life outside the group but with what is going on within the group. Confidentiality thus does not become an issue. Members can use the group process as an arena in which honest, genuine, uncensored feedback is given "I to Thou." Negative reactions may be expressed, but just as many, if not more, positive reactions will probably be expressed. The interaction takes place at a level of intense experiencing together of each passing moment, and the experiencing is described verbally. The functions of modeling, facilitating, and catalyst (Chapter 5) all have as their purpose to maintain the intensity of Cell II material.

Such interactions are appropriate in only a few situations outside a group. If, in routine social intercourse, people were to describe their ongoing reactions to each other at this level of intensity, economic productivity would probably be diminished. Frequent bulletins from "viscera land" become ludicrous, and, unless all concerned are operating from Cell II agendas, the misunderstandings that could occur would be countless and disastrous. Such discussions "in group" are another matter.

The interaction group is unique in that it is the total agenda for each member to obtain honest feedback on how others are experiencing them. This requires that members of a group risk themselves to perform this "act of grace." When members respond to each other out of Cell II, they are giving a part of themselves not usually offered. They are risking rejection and misunderstanding. By lowering their defenses, they become open and vulnerable. Feedback of this kind represents a gift of great value — an act of grace, something of infinite worth, a part of another human being.

This act of grace — giving authentic feedback and receiving the gift of honest reaction — is built on a principle that *must* be transmitted to the group by the leader and then reinforced throughout the life of the group. (The obvious application to life outside the group needs no comment.) This principle is basic to this area of communication: "When I speak, I speak only about me, about my values, about what I feel is good or bad for me. My feedback to you is a statement about me. If I react to you in an assertive or attacking manner, or if I relate to you in a neutral or nonrisking monologue, or if I relate to you in a caring, empathic way, I am communicating how it is with me and I am risking something of my essence."

One of the group leader's traffic-directing functions is to keep this basic principle surfaced in the group processes: that every statement we make, in the final analysis, is about ourselves. For example, if I say, "You are stupid," the statement carries no credence concerning your character nor should it be internalized by you as a reality about *you*. Rather, when I assert that you are stupid, I am speaking from *my* biases, and *my* emotional sets. What I really am saying is that *I* am experiencing frustrations, dislikes of your behavior, and am unable to cope with you at this time. Thus the "you are stupid" statement is really a statement about *me* — not about you; not that I am stupid, but that I see what you are doing as stupid. If you choose to internalize my comments as belonging to you rather than to me, it would diminish both of us. You will have given over your autonomy, and I will have been experienced as judger. Rather, in feedback you might choose to legitimize my feelings as a truth about me — that I am perceiving your behaviors as stupid — and our dialogue can continue with the channels of communication wide open.

Long before the extensional group existed, Buddha recognized this truth: that when a person speaks, he or she speaks only of and for himself or herself. A parable tells the story of a foolish man who, learning that Buddha observed the principle of returning good for evil, came and abused him. Buddha was silent until the man finished. Then he asked him, "If I decline to accept a gift made to me, to whom then does the gift belong?" The man answered, "In that case, it would still belong to the person who offered it." Buddha replied, "Since I decline to accept your abuse, does it not then belong to you?" The man made no reply but walked slowly away, carrying with him that which he had wished to give to another (Siu, 1968).

Conclusion

The Johari Window was not presented for its deep psychological implications but in the hope that the reader will comprehend it as a simple, practical means for organizing common sense. As we begin to recognize simple interactive systems, we also become aware of our expanded choices. We can choose to offer feedback to another person, and we can choose to invite feedback from others. The extent to which we allow ourselves to be known and act to know others is clearly a matter of choice. The manner in which leaders assume their responsibilities and exercise their skills largely determines the kinds of interpersonal choices group members will make.

SUMMARY

Three conceptual frameworks for comprehending interaction among group members have been presented: Jungian

67

typology, FIRO, and Johari Window. Each of the three concepts views interpersonal contact from a different perspective. Jungian typology holds that everyone has a preferred style of interpreting reality. FIRO points out that interpersonal needs differ on an individual basis. Johari Window maintains that interpersonal interaction includes commonly known information between two persons, as well as a degree of knowledge and awareness on the part of each that is independent and unknown to the other. When unknowns are shared (self-disclosure), the probability of trust and interpersonal effort increases.

The three conceptual frameworks provide an intricate weave of human complexity. Group leaders who are ignorant or unappreciative of the complexities of human interaction cannot possibly be effective. The three conceptual frameworks attempt to provide some degree of clarity and organization to consideration of these complexities.

REFERENCES

Jung, Carl. *Psychological Types.* New York: Harcourt, Brace, 1923.

Kiersey, David, and Bates, Marilyn. *Please Understand Me: An Essay on Temperament Styles.* Del Mar, CA: Prometheon Books, 1978.

Luft, Joseph. *Of Human Interaction.* Palo Alto, CA: National Press Books, 1969.

Luft, Joseph, and Ingram, Harry. "The Johari Window, A Graphic Model of Awareness in Interpersonal Relations," in *Group Processes: An Introduction to Group Dynamics.* Palo Alto, CA: National Press Books, 1963, pp. 10-12.

Myers, Isabelle. *Myers-Briggs Type Indicator.* Princeton, NJ: Educational Testing Service, 1962.

Schutz, William C. *FIRO (The Interpersonal Underworld).* Palo Alto, CA: Science and Behavior Books, 1966. (First edition, 1958)

————. *Here Comes Everybody.* New York: Harper and Row, 1971.

_____. *Elements of Encounter*. Big Sur, CA: Joy Press, 1973.

_____. *FIRO-B*. Palo Alto, CA: Consulting Psychologists Press, 1977. (Second edition)

Siu, R. G. H. *The Man of Many Qualities — A Legacy of The I Ching*. Cambridge, MA: MIT Press, 1968, p. 73.

von Franz, Marie-Louise, and Hillman, James. *Jung's Typology*. New York: Spring Publications, 1975.

Yabroff, William W. *Psychological Type Inventory*. Santa Clara, CA: Department of Education, University of Santa Clara, 1978.

4

The Nature and Techniques
of Leaders

4

The Nature and Techniques
of Leaders

THE NATURE OF LEADERS

A group is a mirror of its leader. A group draws definition from its leader. It will be only as good as the leader, as good as his or her skills, and as good as the leader's own being. Leaders may be competent in the technical aspects of group leadership, but if they are not "good" human beings, their groups will usually become destructive — i.e., the group members will be diminished. Whether a leader is working with a remedial group or an extensional group, he or she must be a "nourishing" human being. A leader who is "toxic," as Greenwald (n.d.) suggests, may suck nourishment out of others. A group led by a toxic leader may be unhealthy for participants, whereas a group led by a "nourishing" leader is enriching and growth producing. If, as Greenwald claims, toxic people radiate their deadliness to others, a depressed, hostile leader may radiate depression and hostility throughout a group. A nourishing leader, on the other hand, thrives on joyous human interaction and is a self-nourisher who generates his or her own enrichment rather than feeding off group members.

Maintenance Groups

Greenwald's constructs of toxic and nourishing people imply that it is important for the group leader to belong to a

73

maintenance group in which he or she participates as a group member. If, as Greenwald claims, toxicity is contagious, and groups inevitably contain some toxic members, group leaders must plan a program for the maintenance of their own psychological well-being. We highly recommend that a group be formed for group leaders, for the purpose of maintaining their growth toward self-actualization. A maintenance group of professional group leaders should meet twice monthly and rotate leadership each group session. The agenda would be the continual inward exploration of self to maintain and consolidate personal growth gains.

The Co-leader Model

In a group of convalescing patients, one of the co-leaders and several of the group members were intently involved with one patient/group member who had been refusing to cooperate with the instructions of her physical therapist. She was to walk for a brief period in order to prevent atrophy and, it was hoped, to regain some strength in her legs and hips. The exercise was so painful that the patient chose to stay in her bed or in her wheelchair. Several group members were trying to encourage her to comply with the physical therapist's (one of the co-leaders) program.

As attention continued to be focused on the one uncooperative patient, another member quietly, almost imperceptibly, shook her head "no." Her nonverbal message would have gone undetected had not the other co-leader noticed and asked, "Hilda, your head [movement] suggests that you're not agreeing with something or somebody." Hilda replied sadly, "I wish there had been a group like this last year when I needed encouragement. I was feeling so sorry for myself after my stroke, I gave up. I didn't exercise like I was supposed to, and I'm still here [in the convalescent hospital]."

The writers believe that the co-leader model provides the most effective model of group leadership. This format offers a way to attain productivity in a group with maximum control of the process and a minimum of risk and control of members.

The male-female co-leader model is preferred, but a dyadic model of the same sex may be satisfactory at times. Regardless of sex, the team must be complementary and must work from the same theoretical orientation. Teams who have not worked together previously may experience some difficulty in trusting each other or understanding each other's mode of functioning, but within two sessions those who find the relationship comfortable should have learned to work with each other.

Co-leaders who have had successful experience in this model find it more satisfactory than single leadership. One satisfaction stems from the post-group critique that co-leaders hold. Areas of concern, areas of success, and areas that need to be explored can be discussed by the team immediately after a session. Instant feedback can be given concerning the leadership of the group session.

Another satisfaction with the model lies in the "anchor" one member of the team provides while the other member is engaged in intensive interaction with one or several members of the group. When one group leader focuses deeply into the life-space of an individual member, this leader cannot monitor other group members. In the co-leader model the other leader can maintain this function, thus ensuring the ongoing safety of group members.

A third advantage of the co-leader approach is that it provides a model of confrontation without risking a group member. Co-leaders are expendable to each other and the group and, without being "phony," can use one another to model confrontation early in group life at a depth that might be unwise if the interaction were taking place between leader and member.

A fourth asset of the co-leader model is the constant check each has on the counter-transferences, self-needs, distortions stemming from biases, and the possible inaccuracies and inadequacies of the other. Each co-leader can keep the other "honest" by giving feedback concerning his or her inauthentic behavior.

The co-leaders should position themselves across from one another in the group circle. Either can begin the session. The productivity level of the group can be maintained by the constant interaction of two leaders. Groups led by co-leaders tend to move rapidly and to sustain intense interaction through a session.

According to a study reported in *Frontiers of Hospital Psychiatry* (Herscheiman & Freundich, 1970) concerning the use of co-therapists in large-group therapy, co-leaders were able to keep the sessions from becoming intellectual or dull, and as they became more comfortable working together, to lead one another away from unproductive areas and to sense group affect that might have been missed had they been operating alone. This study found that some leaders were more capable of handling anger, depression, or resistance, while others showed greater skill at being supportive. A major advantage of having more than one group leader was the enhanced ability to penetrate members' resistances and to quickly reach significant affect-laden material. Working together, the co-leaders did not allow members to dwell on areas they knew were unproductive, but could move them to meaningful material rapidly. The use of co-leaders in large-group therapy also was seen as an opportunity to train beginning group leaders by providing them with a setting in which they could work across from an experienced leader.

The dialogues below — one involving a student, one involving an adult member — illustrate the interaction between co-leaders:

Member (Mike):	John, you just burn me up because of your being dishonest all the time.
Co-leader No. 1:	Mike, you seem angry with John. Tell John exactly what you think about him.
Co-leader No. 2:	(To Co-leader No. 1) I am uncomfortable with your statement. You seem to be manipulating Mike against John, and it would be more helpful to me if you shared your feelings.

Member (Lois):	(To Co-leader No. 1) You refuse to deal with my anger and hostilities. You constantly duck the issue and refuse to deal with me.
Co-leader No. 2:	Lois, you're so overwhelmed with your feelings that you can't seem to clarify them. I would like to deal with you and have you tell me what's going on.
Lois:	I can't seem to get any response or emotion from Co-leader No. 1.
Co-leader No. 1:	It seems to me, Lois, that you somehow want me to pick up and swallow your anger and hostility. I react that if I did that, we would both be angry, and I can't see what help that would be to either of us.

THE LEADER'S TECHNIQUES

A leader can possess brilliant techniques but still be ineffective. Techniques are tools that are only as good as the user. The nature of the leader is primary; it is his or her art. The nature of the leader's techniques is secondary; it is his or her science. Some of the verbal dimensions of group interaction that constitute that science are: confrontation, attending behavior, feedback, use of questions, levels of interaction, and opening and closing a session. The four major *functions* of group leaders (traffic director, model, interaction catalyst, communication facilitator) are analyzed in detail in Chapter 5.

Confrontation — An Act of Grace

Confrontation offered with empathy is an act of grace. Confrontation offered with animosity is an act without grace. The line that divides the two lies within the confronter. His or her caring, unconditional, positive regard, congruency, authenticity, *agape* (making no demand in return) render confrontation a gift of great value. Without these characteristics,

77

confrontation can become twisted by hostility and diminish both receiver and sender.

Hill (1965), Bach (1967), and Blaker (1973) have identified confrontation as a helpful dimension in verbal interaction. Anderson (1968) has provided additional understanding of the impact of confrontation. She has found that, *if* the leader operates with a high degree of empathy, with positive regard for the client, genuineness, concreteness, and self-disclosure, the offering or confrontation will be facilitating. If, on the other hand, the leader operates at low levels of empathy, does not truly care for the client, and is inauthentic and fearful of risking himself or herself, confrontation will be experienced by the client as criticizing, unfeeling, and overly intellectual. Leaders who consistently operate at a high level of interaction tend to respond to the strengths and resources of a client, while leaders who tend to function at a low level respond to the member's weaknesses.

The benchmark of confrontation is the risk leaders take with themselves in making the verbal offering. In confrontation they state clearly their position, feelings, perceptions; they state them in the here and now; and they are discrepant with those offered by the member. For example, a member might say, "I couldn't do my homework again last night because the teacher didn't make it clear, and I forgot to take my book home anyway. Besides, there was too much noise in the house because my dad and mom were looking at TV." A confrontation might be, "I'm feeling pretty irritated by your comment. I think you're blaming everyone else and never intended to do the work." In this confrontation the member knows that the leader disagrees with him and feels a little angry at that moment, but the member also knows that the leader cared enough to risk herself in a way that could have caused the member to reject her and turn on her in anger.

The purpose in confronting is to share perceptions and to communicate authentically — *not* to prove one's point. The leader must keep this purpose in mind when helping members confront each other. Confrontation is not intended to identify the "right" view or to establish one's superiority over another.

Attackers are trying to win or to dominate. In confrontation, the information being offered could easily have been concealed rather than shared. Confrontation means providing another person with a different perspective from which to view a problem or revealing observed behavior of which another person is unaware. Confrontation is a caring act. It is also a form of feedback. What the recipient does with the feedback is entirely up to him or her.

Confronting a speaker who generalizes excessively is also helpful at times in maintaining group interaction.

In a high school group a student had made the remark that no one in the whole world really cared what his thoughts and opinions were. Another student confronted the speaker with, "Hey man, wait a minute. You've included me as someone who doesn't care — and that simply ain't so. I care about you and what's important to you.

A leader who engages in confrontation is taking a risk and knows it. The confronter cannot always be certain how others will respond to the information being presented. A leader who confronts a member with his or her perception risks being misunderstood. The member may feel demeaned although the leader did not intend to do that. Often, members may put more stock in a leader's perception than in a fellow group member's because they perceive the leader's status as reinforcing (Blaker, 1976, p. 11). What the leader says may be interpreted as "fact," but stating "facts" is not the purpose of confrontation. The leader must model confronting behavior and must be prepared to review the subjective nature of confrontation as often as may be necessary to help the group.

Confrontation, then, represents a more intense and important form of feedback in that the speaker (the confronter) assumes responsibility for what is being shared. Our perceptions can be only tentative and subjective. Normally, perceptions change as additional information is provided and experience is gained. That is why confrontation in group interaction is so

79

valuable. Group leaders or members who are willing to share their perceptions are offering information to which the receiver does not normally have access — someone's perception of him or her. We reiterate that what one does with the information, whether it alters one's attitude or behavior, is entirely up to the receiver. Confrontation is *not* offered to force change in the receiver. It is offered as a gift.

Confrontation differs from interpretation, because interpretation means that the leader is making an observation based on some theoretical postulate or inference. For example, if the leader had wished to interpret the member's comment about his homework, she might have said, "I think you are rationalizing all around the issue. You are giving *good* reasons, but not the real ones." Interpretation often tends to focus on the past (a search for explanations of behaviors in previous occurrences) whereas confrontation always focuses on the present moment. Both confrontation and interpretation, however, consist of content to which members can react emotionally and thus, perhaps, gain insight into their own functioning.

Anderson (1968, p. 411) stated that a confrontation can be said to have occurred if:

> 1. The client describes himself to the therapist in terms of what he wishes to be (his ego-ideal) rather than what he is (his real self), whereupon the therapist faces the client with his own experience of the situation.
> 2. The client expresses an increased awareness of himself (insight) as if this were the magical solution to all his problems; that is, there is a discrepancy between the client's insights and his actions in relation to these insights.

Confrontation is an act of grace. In this process the confronter takes a risk, but in so doing sends a message to the receiver that he or she, the confronter, cares enough to take that risk and respects the integrity and self-determination of the receiver. The confronter is saying, "I respect you, I value you, and I believe you have the strength to receive me fully — uncensored and giving all of myself, my reactions, and my perceptions. Knowing that you may reject me, I am giving you some of my essence. I do this because I care for you."

Two dialogues serve to represent confrontation in group interaction:

Dick:	I don't like you, Mary. You are a manipulating female, and you make me mad.
Mary:	Dick, I experience you as using me to get rid of your hostilities toward women, and I don't like you to do that, because I want your acceptance and caring.

Ken:	That dumb teacher picks on me all the time.
Edsel:	Aw, Ken, you bring it on yourself, and because I care for you, I get mad when you make statements like that. You cause the trouble and you try to blame the teacher. I would like to help you if I can.

Attending Behavior

Group leaders may not be aware of some of their nonverbal messages, particularly those that transmit attending or non-attending behavior. The use of video-tape recordings can help increase the leader's awareness of this kind of behavior.

Ivey, et al. (1968) have used attending behavior as their initial focus in microcounseling — working with the one-to-one relationship — but their observations are relevant to the leader's work. Three focal points of attending behavior have been identified with both verbal and nonverbal components.

The first is *eye contact*. If a group leader does not maintain eye contact with his or her members, they are likely to feel they are being treated as objects rather than subjects. A major vehicle for transmitting empathy is eye contact; thus, group leaders should be acutely aware of what they are doing with their eye "language."

A second component of attending behavior includes *postural movement and gestures*. A group leader can transmit the message, "I hear, I understand, I feel," through body posture.

The third element, *verbal following behavior*, also transmit attending or nonattending. Beginning leaders have difficulty "tracking" accurately the outputs of a member in a one-to-one relationship, and it is infinitely more difficult to track accurately the outputs of members of a group. Nonetheless, this is what group leaders must do, and they must respond in a way that allows group members to know they are being heard. Leaders should respond easily in a variety of modes: reflection of content, reflection of feeling, clarification, and general leads.

Nonverbal cues are discussed more thoroughly in Chapter 6.

Feedback

The giving and receiving of feedback is the life stream of a group. Without it, the group has no reason for existing. Yet, the leader cannot assume that members are sensitive to this kind of communication. Generally in our dailiy lives we receive little feedback, and almost never the honest kind that is the *sine qua non* of group life. Without feedback, we blindly continue making the same mistakes day after day. Even though we may be dimly aware that something is amiss in our behavior, we are seldom able to specify exactly which behaviors are causing our discomfort. We do not know just what we are doing that causes unwanted reactions in others. Consequently, we do not possess the raw materials of change — the awareness of unwanted behaviors.

It is no accident that we do not routinely give and receive feedback in our daily lives. Doing so is extremely difficult, and it involves a personal risk that most people are not willing to take. It also involves a commitment to another human being, which is indeed rare. And it requires a skill not commonly possessed.

If group members are to learn how to give and receive feedback, group leaders must transmit this information through modeling in their own behavior and, perhaps, through direct instruction. One tool that is provided in this book to help teach group members to give and receive feedback is "The Open Letter" (see Appendix B). Leaders may wish to reinforce the concepts contained in this letter early in the life of the group.

Feedback is not always helpful. Leaders have to be alert to the motives behind members' feedback offerings. Often the material is rejecting rather than confrontive, and the primary motivation of the member who is giving the feedback is to punish another group member in some way or to make the giver of the feedback feel better. If such situations occur, the leader is responsible for calling attention to his or her own reaction to the feedback and questioning the member's motives. Also, members may engage in "groupie" behavior in the guise of feedback, using their verbalizations to demonstrate how sophisticated, perceptive, or brilliant they are.

Then again, feedback may be motivated by a caring for someone else and a willingness to share oneself, despite the risk this entails. Authentic feedback (Holden, 1969), like confrontation, is an act of grace.

Feedback must be specific to be helpful, and it must deal with behaviors that are *current* and that can be changed. For example, if one member comments to another, "I think you are very unfriendly," the leader might ask the commenting member to specify exactly what behaviors of this "unfriendly" member gave rise to such an impression. (And, as always, the leader emphasizes that in all our statements we are essentially talking about ourselves!)

Feedback should be verbalized so that it is clearly related to the frame of reference of the person offering the feedback. Thus, "I am getting tense sitting next to you because you have been tapping your foot for several minutes," would be preferable to, "You are tense tonight. What is the matter?" Early in a group's life the leader may have to intervene frequently to insist that speakers talk from their own point of view — where *they* are — rather than focus their comments on the member who is the target of the feedback. As members learn how to give self-centered feedback, the leader will have to intervene much less frequently.

83

Feedback must not be perceived as a mandate for change. Again and again the leader must emphasize that givers of feedback are describing how it is with them and that the receiver may do with the comments whatever he or she chooses. If receivers of feedback choose to change, it must be because *they* want to, not because a member of the group "suggests" that they do so. Every member should be helped to realize that no one has the right to ask another to change. *Feedback only transmits information about how it is with the sender; it does not solicit changes on the part of the receiver.*

A curious situation often occurs in the giving of "pseudo-feedback." One member might comment to another, "I used to find you cold and unfeeling, but now I find you warmer," and then wait expectantly for a response. The receiving person inevitably feels that a burden is placed on him or her and that he or she is expected to do something with it. In actuality, this person is left with nothing to say except an inane, "That's nice" or a rude, "So?" or an uncomfortable, "I like you, too." The original comment was a subtle form of "groupie" behavior that is difficult for a leader to handle without seeming to reprimand. The leader could call attention to the comment's hook of when-did-you-stop-beating-your-wife, or intervene with a comment about how the pseudo-feedback made the leader feel. The giver of the pseudo-feedback probably had good intentions, but this kind of interaction is *not* authentic feedback — which must have a handle on it that will enable the receiver to deal with it and respond to it.

Using the foregoing example, real feedback might have gone like this: "I feel bad that I used to see you as cold and un-caring and would like to ask for your understanding of my blind spot." In this case the receiver is left with a handle by which to respond, and the interaction can continue. (The behavior of "problem" members is discussed further in Chapter 7.)

Group interaction is based on feedback. The effectiveness of a group depends on the quality of the feedback contained in the group's interaction, and the group leader is responsible for controlling the quality of that feedback. From honest, helpful feedback group members may gain self-understanding and an increased awareness of the effects of certain of their behaviors on others; they may become more sensitive to contradictions between their verbal and nonverbal messages; they may come to understand distortions in their communication patterns; they may experience a heightened sense of self as delightful, exciting, warm, and loving human beings.

Here are three examples of feedback dialogue:

Leslie:	I wish someone would help me understand how I'm coming on "child."
Clarence:	You ask questions when you really know the answer.
Don:	You sit in a little-girl way . . .
Leader (to Don):	It would be helpful if you were more specific.
Don:	Well, Leslie, you fold your hands in your lap, and you tip your head to one side when you are coming on "child."

Bob:	I don't like coming to you [the leader] because you never seem to have time for me. I put in a request, and what you do I don't know because I don't get to see you.
Co-leader No. 1:	Bob, you are attacking me, and I don't know what to say.
Co-leader No. 2 to Co-leader No. 1:	I experience you as being on the spot and not knowing how to handle it. Some feedback about how you are feeling might be helpful.

George:	I tried out for the football team, but the coach has favorites and I can't ever get to play.

> *Sandy:* George, you hardly ever turn up for practice, you fool around during line-up, you don't follow team rules — I don't really think you can make it, and this is your way of getting out of it.

Misuse of Questions as a Technique

Leaders must be equipped to control the group process, but leaders must *not* control the group members. The trap inherent in the use of questions as a leadership technique is that questions *do* control group members (Passons, 1975, p. 90; Lalanne, 1975). The most efficient method of keeping members in submission is to interrogate them. In this way a leader can appear to be the "authority" who seeks information from others without revealing too much of himself or herself. Leaders can exercise iron control over members through firing questions at them, particularly "why" questions (Passons, 1975, p. 92). If the leader engages in this kind of questioning, members experience themselves as objects, and the leader relates to them as things to be manipulated, not as persons to be known.

It is probably more difficult for leaders to eliminate questions from their own verbal behavior than it is to eliminate questions from group members. Leaders who give up questions may be giving up their own method of control — their entire repertoire of group leadership techniques.

To eliminate questions from members, all the leader has to do is insist that members rephrase questions into statements, making clear their positions. For example, a member might query another member, "Why didn't you ask the teacher for permission to leave the room?" The leader's responsibility is to intervene and insist that the member asking the question make a statement concerning his or her position, thought, or assumption behind the question. In response to the leader's request that the thought behind the question be made clear, the questioner might say, "I think you should have asked the teacher for permission to leave the room." Again the "hook" of the question has been turned into a "handle" to which a receiver can respond.

Leaders should permit questions either on their own part or on the part of group members *only* when the asker needs the information, such as, "Are we meeting next Tuesday?" Leaders also should be aware that questions tend to probe into the private life-space, Cell III of the Johari Window (see Chapter 3). Even such a simple question as, "What did you do last night?" may trespass into that space, and the leader should intervene by asking the questioner to volunteer where *he* or *she* is here and now, rather than volunteering another member's life-space.

Opening a Session

Leaders need to have some general leads at their command to use in opening sessions. These might be: "We can begin anywhere you like," "Let's get started," or "It's time to begin." These statements simply give the signal that the group is in session.

Group leaders also may want to use some of the confrontation techniques, both verbal and nonverbal (see Chapter 8), to begin a group, but there is a danger that the group will become dependent on the leader always to initiate interaction. If leaders allow this to happen, they are depriving members of the opportunity to develop independence and autonomy. Therefore, if leaders choose to use some interaction stimulators in one session, they should not take complete responsibility for initiating interaction in the next.

Leaders also may begin a group with silence, waiting for a member to initiate verbal communication. The danger in this is that the silence can become punitive. If it does, leaders have the responsibility for breaking the silence. They might do so by sharing where *they* are and how *they* feel. Leaders have no more right to volunteer a member than one member has the right to volunteer another. The only legitimate tools leaders possess to model here-and-now behaviors are themselves (or the co-leaders). This is not to imply that leaders ever become members of their groups — they are *always* the leaders; they are there for the gain of the members. Leaders must join their own growth or maintenance groups if they wish to become members.

The "go-around" is helpful to open a session. The leader may suggest, for example, a go-around in which each member shares how he or she is feeling at that very minute. After making the original suggestion, the leader may continue to comment for a few seconds, having made clear where the go-around will begin and the direction it will take. The leader can initiate the experience by sharing of himself or herself, asking for feedback, thus modeling group membership behavior. Then he or she may encourage the others to participate. The reason for the delay between the suggestion and implementation is to give members a moment to prepare themselves, to marshal their thoughts — in other words, to avoid surprises that generate defensive reactions.

Beginning group leaders often make the mistake of assuming that a group will begin one session right where the last session ended. This is a faulty assumption. When a group parts, each member (and the leader) continues the internal dialogue with self for many hours. During these "self-conversations" growth takes place, insights occur, understandings develop. Thus, it is naive to assume that a group will begin where it ended. Rather, leaders should assume that the group members are in quite a different place from where they were when they left off. Leaders should attempt to begin each session, then, in the here and now, making no assumptions about the there and then.

Closing a Session

Groups must begin and end on time. Through groups, members test and learn limits, and if leaders exceed the agreed-upon limits, they are abdicating their responsibility and reinforcing a perception many group members may already have —that people often don't mean what they say, that they cannot be trusted. The same rationale applies to the number of sessions.

An eight-session group is just that — not an eight-plus-two-plus? group. Neophyte group leaders may have difficulty beginning and ending an individual group session on time and terminating the group itself, but, as they gain experience, they come to realize the importance of doing both.

Capping

To end at a previously agreed time, leaders need a technique to bring the group back to the nongroup world — the real, outside world. They do this through *capping*. Somewhere near the end of a session leaders should begin to ease up interaction. Emotional content should be tapered off and cognitive processes made dominant. Leaders do this by responding deliberately to *ideas* and *generalities*, to cognitive rather than conative content. Leaders may talk about the there and then instead of the here and now. They may talk about things and people not present. Thus, the group is brought away from deep emotional exploration toward preparation to function in their usual life-spaces in the world of social reality. The amount of time the leader requires for this process depends on the sophistication of the group, the destination of members when they leave the group (e.g., home, classroom, job, lunch), and the depths of interaction at which the group was working.

Leaders may not wish to cap every group, but they always have to make sure that no member is left in a state of crisis. No member should leave a group session unable to cope with his or her world. At the same time, leaders do not want to close the door on a member's growth, which (unfortunately) may involve some discomfort. The leaders' art of group leadership must be brought into play to help them know when a member is being left in a state of crisis or with an unresolved concern on which he or she needs to work. Leaders with an obsessive need for closure may have difficulty making this decision.

At the end of every session, the leader may wish to cap by giving each member an opportunity to make a final comment. A member may want to direct a remark to a particular member or to the group as a whole or he may not wish to speak. At this point the leader should not stimulate interaction but respond only if it is absolutely necessary.

A leader may wish to have members write logs at the end of every session. Index cards titled "Group Reflections" could be used. The cards should be signed so the leader can keep in touch with each member. These logs are rarely read aloud to the group or referred to in the group.

Levels of Interaction

Carkhuff and Berenson (1967) identified five levels of responses with the one-to-one counseling relationship in mind, but these levels seem to apply to the group leader's functioning as well. The levels range from one, the lowest level, to five, the most accurate level of interaction.

At Level 1 a response indicates either that the group leader did not attend to the communication of a member or that the leader's response detracted significantly from the member's expression. For example, a member might say, "I just can't seem to get along with my wife." A Level 1 response from the leader might be, "Where does she work?"

At Level 2 the leader's responses subtract noticeably from the feelings communicated by a member. Thus, in response to the comment, "I just can't get along with my wife," the leader might reply, "How long have you two been married?"

At Level 3 the leader's response adds to the statement of a member, but it is essentially interchangeable with the member's comment and does not help the member understand what he or she is really saying. In response to, "I just can't get along with my wife," the leader might say, "The two of you just seem to be at odds." In this case, the leader's and member's remarks had essentially the same affect and the same meaning, but the leader's statement did not subtract from that of the member.

In Level 4 responses the leader adds to the expressions of members in such a way as to express feelings that are a level deeper than those expressed by the member. To "I just can't seem to get along with my wife," the leader might respond,

"You are feeling pretty despondent about the whole situation and don't quite know what to do about it." The leader "heard" the feelings the member did not verbalize and responded to them.

At Level 5 the leader's remarks add significantly to the feelings and meanings of members by accurately expressing levels of feeling deeper than the members are able to express. In responding to the example, "I just can't seem to get along with my wife," the leader might say, "I'm feeling almost a panic in you, a feeling of being closed in, pushed from all sides, trapped, and going under deeper."

Carkhuff and Berenson's work (1967) is especially important in that they have pointed out that leaders who are not functioning at a more facilitative level than members will harm the members. If this is the case in the one-to-one relationship, it is logical to assume that this is also true of the group leader's relationship with his or her members. It also may be true for the interrelationships among members. If this *is* the case, the necessity for group leaders to be able to control the group process cannot be overemphasized.

SUMMARY

This chapter has discussed the nature of the group leader, emphasizing the importance of the leader's own personal level of interaction and its implications for his or her ability to provide human nourishment. The co-leader paradigm was advanced as the most effective model in achieving maximum group productivity in a minimum amount of time.

The nature of the group leader's techniques was discussed in relation to the level of interaction, use of confrontation, components of attending behaviors, use and misuse of feedback as the *sine qua non* of group life, and misuse of questions as a technique. A discussion of procedures for opening and closing sessions and a section on capping also were included.

REFERENCES

Anderson, Susan C. "Effects of Confrontation by High-and-Low-Functioning Therapists," *Journal of Counseling Psychology*, Vol. 15, No. 5 (1968), pp. 411-16.

Bach, George. "Marathon Group Dynamics: Dimensions of Helpfulness," *Psychological Reports 20*, Southern Universities Press, 1967, pp. 1147-58.

Blaker, Kenneth E. "Confrontation," in Anita Mitchell and Clarence D. Johnson (Eds.), *Therapeutic Techniques: Working Models for The Helping Profession*. Fullerton: California Personnel and Guidance Association, 1973.

———*Behavior Modification*. Morristown, NJ: General Learning Press, 1976.

Carkhuff, Robert R., and Berenson, Bernard G. *Beyond Counseling and Therapy*. New York: Holt, Rinehart, and Winston, 1967.

Greenwald, Jerry A. "The Art of Emotional Nourishment: Self Induced Nourishment and Toxicity." Unpublished manuscript, Jerry Greenwald, Ph.D., 450 N. Bedford Drive, Beverly, Hills, CA (n.d.).

Herscheiman, Philip, and Freundich, David. "Large Group Therapy Seen as an Improvement Over Ward Meetings," *Frontiers of Hospital Psychiatry*, Vol. 7, No. 11 (1970).

Hill, William F. *Hill Interaction Matrix*. Los Angeles: University of Southern California Press, 1965.

Holden, George. "On Openness and Authenticity," *The School Counselor*, September 1969, pp. 4-9.

Ivey, Allen E., Normington, Cheryl J., Miller, C. Dean, Morrill, Weston H., and Haase, Richard R. "Microcounseling and Attending Behavior: An Approach to Prepracticum Counselor Training, *Journal of Counseling Psychology*, Vol. 15, No. 5, Part 2 (September 1968), Monograph Supplement.

Lalanne, Jacques. "Attack by Question," *Psychology Today*, Vol. 9, No. 6 (November 1975), p. 134.

Passons, William R. *Gestalt Approaches to Counseling*. New York: Holt, Rinehart, and Winston, 1975.

5

A Microanalysis of The Four Functions of Group Leadership

- Traffic Director
  - Blocking Questions
  - Blocking Gossip
  - Blocking the There-and-Then
    - Presentizing
    - Personalizing
  - Blocking Super-mothering
  - Blocking Mind-raping
  - Blocking Invasion of Privacy
- Model
- Interaction Catalyst
- Communication Facilitator
  - Reflective Listening
    - Reflecting Content
    - Reflecting Feelings
  - Linking
  - Speaking Congruently ("I" Messages)
  - Perception Checking
  - The Eyes of the Leaders
  - The Ears of the Leaders
  - Communication Patterns to Avoid
- Summary

5

A Microanalysis of The Four Functions
of Group Leadership

The role of the extensional leader is characterized by professional expertise coupled with clear acceptance of the responsibility of leadership. The person of the leader, in the final analysis, defines the role. Who he or she is — his or her authenticity, awareness, degree of self-actualization, empathy, intelligence, self-acceptance, in short "human-ness" — is the most relevant variable that this person brings to group leadership (Dreyfus, 1967). Without these sensitivities, professional expertise is gratuitous. Without professional expertise, the sensitivities are also gratuitous. A knowledge of the functions of group leadership is essential preparation for the role of leaders and co-leaders.

These functions are analyzed in detail in this chapter. A "micro approach" has been taken to isolate the components, but the functions interrelate, complementing and supplementing one another. The whole of group leadership and co-leadership is a great deal more than the sum of the components — a symbiotic relationship. Leaders must each go through their own process of synthesizing and integrating these functions into a gestalt. The intent of this chapter is to specify the four micro-elements that seem to the writers to comprise the gestalt of co-leadership (the preferred model of these authors). The roles are those of: traffic-director; model; interaction catalyst; and communication facilitator.

TRAFFIC DIRECTOR

One function that requires active attention early in a group's life is traffic-directing. Leaders have to help members become aware of behaviors that open communication channels and those that inhibit communication. As members learn group membership responsibility, traffic-directing interventions of the leaders diminish. The few that are required after the first sessions are usually performed by the members themselves.

Blocking Questions

A vital traffic-directing function, one that meets with the most resistance, is that of blocking questions (Passons, 1975). Out-of-group speech patterns rely heavily on the questioning form of communication. The awareness that a questioner controls the responder in a subtle way is only dimly perceived by most people. Group members tend to bring to the group a heavy reliance on questions as a way of communicating. Leaders take away this self-protective, defensive "crutch" when they ask a member to abandon his or her traditional way of controlling others through the "hooks" of questions, and to come out in the open with a clear statement of what he or she really means to say. At first the member inevitably feels angry and hostile and evidences impatience and resistance. Leaders have to determine when the price of intervention in terms of irritation to members is likely to be inhibiting or facilitating, and use their judgments as to when to intervene and when to abstain. The blocking of questions must be done gently, without rejecting the questioner.

Two examples might be:

Member:
(John):   Why do you feel like that, Paul?

Leader   John, you have phrased your concern so
(intervention): that Paul doesn't know how it is with you.
                   I feel it will be more helpful if you make it
                   clear what you have in mind.

John:	Paul, I guess I don't relate to what you're saying because I don't think I would feel that way.
	(John's first statement implies judgment. His second statement is a clear message of where he stands concerning the issue and with Paul.)

Member (Mary):	How do you feel about it, Ralph?
Leader (intervention):	I wish you would make it clear to Ralph how you feel about it, Mary.
Mary:	You make me mad, Ralph. I want you to say how you feel about the situation, and I'm irritated with you because you haven't.

Blocking Gossip

Blocking "gossip" is far easier than blocking questions. To block questions, the leader must work against an ingrained speech pattern that involves a valued control of others. In situations involving gossip, members are talking *about* another member rather than directly *to* the member. For example, one member may refer to something that occurred, or a reaction, or a concern that involves another member, and addresses still another member or the group as a whole. In such a situation the leader should intervene and ask the member to speak directly to the other member concerned.

Leaders' interventions to block gossip are inherently inconsistent. When they direct one member to speak directly to another member, rather than speaking about him or her, leaders are themselves speaking *about* the other member. This problem seems imbedded in the English language and appears to be a necessary case of "Don't do as I do, but as I say" on the part of the intervening leader. One way to handle this inconsistency is to call the group's attention to the necessity for the leader's intervention being stated in the third person while asking members to communicate in the first person.

Examples of gossip in the content of the group multilogue might be:

Joe:	Pete, I am mad at you now for doing those silly things.
Bill (to Joe):	Joe, I am mad at Pete, too.
Leader (intervention):	Bill, you are talking *about* Pete. Please talk directly to him.
Bill:	Pete, I am mad at you too, and would like you to quit doing the things that you later regret.

Mary:	John didn't really mean what he said, I'm sure.
Leader (intervention):	Mary, would you please speak directly to John.
Mary:	John, I don't think that you really meant that comment to be destructive.

Blocking the There and Then

In helping members focus on the here and now, leaders may have to continue their traffic directions periodically throughout the life of the group. Some participants seem able to learn quickly to exist in the present time and place. Others need direction from the leaders or members to relate their comments to the here-and-now group life. Two techniques are available for accomplishing this — *presentizing* and *personalizing* (Passons, 1975).

Presentizing

Some there-and-then content may be appropriate, but leaders should constantly monitor this content for its current relevancy. What do a member's verbalizations mean to him or her right now? What is he or she saying to another member right now? Interventions by leaders refocus mind sets on the immediate experiencing of members, away from reliving the past or rehearsing the future.

Personalizing

As members talk about the there-and-then world, they tend to talk in generalities, using "we," "people," "all of us," and "they," rather than to take full responsibility for their comments by speaking in the first person. Appealing to the authority of the majority is a common way by which people control one another. A leader must intervene in group so that members learn to indicate clearly their responsibility for their own statements. The prelude to taking responsibility is to recognize first those habitual speech patterns that shift authority to others. A representative dialogue may illustrate these points:

Sue:	Last week, during group, I was really shook up at the apathy this group has toward people's problems.
Leader (presentizing intervention):	And apparently you still have some feelings about it now.
Sue:	Yeah, as a group we haven't helped each other at all.
Leader (personalizing intervention):	It seems to me, Sue, that you can only talk for yourself. You may want to share your thoughts.

99

Sue:	Okay. I don't feel that I've been helped by anyone here at all, and I wish someone would help me.
Leader (presentizing intervention):	Would you be more specific, please. Maybe there is someone in particular that you have in mind . . . here . . . now.
Sue:	Yeah . . . you, John, and you, Mary, and you, Pete — I wish each of you would give me something about what it is that might make people think I don't care about them. That's the message I've been getting from you three, and I'm disturbed by it. I guess I've also been saying that the *group* doesn't care . . . and I think that's what you've been telling me.
Leader:	Understand, Sue — John, Mary, and Pete are individuals. They can only speak for themselves. *They* are not the *group*.
Pete:	I would like to respond, Sue, and give you some feedback on how you have come across to me . . .

Blocking Super-mothering

"Super-mothering" is not restricted to the female sex. Males, as well as females, often intervene in confrontations in an effort to assuage hostility, guilts, and pain. This has also been referred to as "Red Crossing" or "band-aiding." Although the super-mothering is done in an apparent effort to be helpful, it is actually highly manipulative. Probably few members recognize their interventions as motivated by their own inability to confront these emotions, that doing something for someone always has an element of manipulation in the act.

Often in group, one member may be engaged in a confrontation with himself or herself or with another member when another participant interjects a "soothing" comment. The intensity of the confrontation may be lessened and may even be diverted by the super-mothering behavior. But the member may thus be denied the opportunity to face some intra- or interpersonal conflict that might be a source of growth for him or her. The leader should divert the super-mothering intervention so the confrontation may be completed to resolution. This concept is illustrated by:

John:	Jim, when you shake your finger at me like that, I get all tight inside.
Mary (to John):	Jim doesn't mean anything by it. He's just making a point.
Leader:	Mary, you are denying John's feelings. John is saying something he wants Jim to hear.

or

Mae:	I feel betrayed. I believed him and now I know he lied to me. I guess I'm partly angry because I see myself as being taken advantage of and made a fool of.
Mary:	Well, Mae, we all have felt that way at times. I think everybody is made a fool of at one time or another. I remember once when my friend . . .
Leader:	Excuse me, Mary. Mae is talking about something that is important to her. *(To Mae)* You were saying, Mae, that you are feeling angry and foolish about being deceived.

101

Blocking Mind-raping

One of the most difficult interventions to make is that of calling attention to the dynamic in which one participant makes assumptions about what another is thinking or feeling. Members who are thus "interpreted" are negated and illegitimatized. Their minds are raped, and they are likely unaware of the process. As leaders perform their traffic-directing functions, they may bring into awareness that a rape has occurred.

Mind-raping may be confused with feedback. The difference is subtle, but in the latter a participant is "reading" another's thoughts while in the former the participant delivering feedback is putting full responsibility on the other.

An example of mind-raping is:

Maria:	I wish I could like you, Henry, but I always have a feeling of wanting to get away when I'm with you.
Henry (mind-raping):	That's because you think I'm judging you.
Leader:	Henry, you're putting thoughts into Maria's mind and throwing the responsibility onto her.
Henry:	Okay, Maria, I guess I can't speak for what is in your mind, but when I am with you this is how I feel. I . . . (etc.)

A more subtle example is:

Maria:	When I am with you, Henry, I have a need to get away from you . . . I feel uneasy . . .
Henry (mind-raping):	Yeah, you have uneasiness in the stomach, you have fears of being with me, you have unrecognized sexual responses, and you really would like to confront me, but you can't.

Leader: Henry, you have put words to feelings that you only assume Maria has. I'd rather hear how it is with Maria from Maria.

Here's another example:

Maria: When I am with you Henry, I feel . . .

Henry: Mm-hmm, uneasy, uptight, like you would not want to be there, anxious . . .

Leader: Henry, you interrupted Maria, and have not allowed her to finish how it is with her.

Blocking Invasion of Privacy

One of the major traffic-directing functions of leaders is to protect the privacy of members. Questions comprise one speech pattern that may result in the invasion of privacy. The technique of question-blocking has already been addressed in this chapter. The leader also functions as traffic-director by blocking content that may invade privacy. In adult groups, members can safely volunteer materials from their own life-spaces and can exercise judgment as to what to bring to group and what they wish to avoid. When a group consists of minors drawn from a school setting, the protection of privacy becomes more complex. Students *must* have their family's privacy, as well as their own, protected, but young people frequently do not have the judgment to know whether or not content is appropriate to bring to a group.

The leader must be alert to any content that may damage group members or their families, particularly in the school setting. For example, if a student group member who is a minor brings up a concern regarding his or her homosexuality, the leader should immediately block elaboration of the content. Leaders obviously cannot prevent such material from being brought up, but they can avoid further discussion by focusing on other areas.

103

Likewise, a student group member may wish to describe a parental quarrel. This material should *not* be pursued; rather the privacy of the mother and father must be protected. Leaders should focus on concerns and feelings members are experiencing in the here and now.

During a group session with high school girls, one of the girls became quite upset as she began to describe a bitter fight between her parents that she witnessed that morning before leaving for school. Her voice faltered and she appeared to be suppressing tears as she started to describe the intimate and awful details of her sad experience.

The group leader redirected her awareness to what she was experiencing at the very moment that she was speaking. "You must have some pretty bad feelings to have two people fighting who are very important in your life. Can you tell us what your feelings are right now?" The girl began to reveal her feelings of helplessness and despair. Other girls in the group described the feelings they had had in situations that seemed similar to them. They also shared their feelings of support and sympathy for the girl in her moment of sadness.

Privacy is one of the major content differences in individual and group counseling. Areas dealing with family relationships, atypical sexuality, and people not present are *not* appropriate in an extensional group setting, but they are appropriate for exploration in individual counseling. When these content areas come up in the group context, leaders should not further the discussion but, as inconspicuously as possible, suggest that the matter be discussed on a one-to-one basis. A general principle to follow is that the exploration or discussion of any content that may later damage members or their families must not be encourgaed in group.

Examples:

Sally: My mother and father really got into it last night. He came home drunk as usual . . .

Leader (intervention):	I am reacting right now with some tension to your rapid speech and facial scowls, Sally.
Sally:	Yeah, I really feel uptight. I'm tense and would kind of like to yell.

Jim:	I'm kind of mixed up. I had a dream last night that I was in a show and a queer sat down next to me. I didn't know what to do.
Leader (intervention):	Dreams are sometimes confusing, Jim. I would like you and I to get together later and talk about it.

MODEL

The interventions of the foregoing dialogues combined elements of the traffic-directing function, in which the leader intervened to focus on the here and now in a participant's personal frame of reference, blocking family problems, sexual problems, and the there and then that dealt with individuals outside the group. These interventions also illustrate the function of modeling. The leader in the examples used himself as a model, verbalizing his own reactions to the speakers. He communicated to the group where he was, how he was feeling, what he was thinking, and, in the process, took full responsibility for his own verbalizations.

When a leader is performing the function of modeling, members may at times assume that the leader is being another member. When leaders transmit how it is with them, group members are not always aware — and need not be aware — that the purpose is to provide a model of authentic interaction. It is not necessary for the members to differentiate between these leadership-membership roles, but it is vital that the leaders do so.

The modeling function involves a leader working in the framework of the extensional model, remaining in the here and now, avoiding use of questions, honoring and protecting the private life-spaces of members, emphasizing positive elements rather than negative elements, being authentic and open, relating to members I-to-Thou, and transmitting a stance of "I'm okay, you're okay" (Harris, 1969). Leaders also model the verbal vehicles that make group processes unique — confrontation and feedback. They teach by example how to be a group member; they do not "teach" group membership by talking about it.

A dialogue illustrating modeling follows:

Joe: I like people very much, and I want to be liked. I find it hard to talk to people I don't know.

Mary: I was wondering if you were ever going to talk, Joe.

Leader: Joe, I feel good that you participated in the group tonight. I like hearing about your feelings.

Another example of modeling:

Gerry: I really react to you, Ada, when you smile. It makes me feel warm and accepted.

Leader: Yes, I can relate to that, Gerry. I respond the same way, Ada. When you smile at me, I feel recognized and legitimatized and very much okay. I like that.

INTERACTION CATALYST

Just as the modeling function overlaps the traffic-directing function, so does the modeling function overlap the interaction catalyst function. To activate group processes, leaders do certain things for certain purposes. They serve as interaction catalysts so that the process will begin to move, people will get involved at a productive level, movement to confrontation will be aided, values will be examined, and awareness of self will be heightened.

Leaders usually serve as interaction catalysts at the beginning of a session. They use, if necessary, some technique to help participants move from the work and social world into the unique world of group. As a group learns membership skills and responsibilities, the leader may not have to continue functioning as catalyst. Group members will soon be able to plunge into a working level without help. At such times, of course, leaders model, traffic-direct, and aid communication, but they do not have to catalyze interaction.

When leaders do choose to use an interaction catalyst technique, they may or may not choose to model that technique. A general guide to keep in mind is that the leader models only for the benefit of the group participants. Thus, if a technique has to be demonstrated in order to be effective, the leader is performing a modeling function.

For instance, if co-leaders wish to activate interaction by using the technique of asking each member to find a concrete object in the immediate environment to which he or she can relate in a personal way, these leaders will probably choose to begin the "go-around" by modeling. One co-leader will present his or her object to the group and try to communicate the elements that he or she sees the object representing. The other co-leader will invite feedback to the co-leader who has been modeling, and then begin the interaction in the group by asking for volunteers. If, at this point, no other member feels comfortable about volunteering, the second co-leader can model, using his or her object. If after feedback has been generated to the second presentation, no member volunteers, the co-leaders may choose to remain silent until members pick up their responsibility to the group and begin interacting.

Chapter 8 includes examples of the interaction catalyst function. Thus, no dialogue is presented in this section.

COMMUNICATION FACILITATOR

A final micro-function of group leadership that can be identified and learned is that of communication facilitator. Some functions of a leader as communication facilitator have already been addressed, but additional facilitating behaviors are discussed here.

As communication facilitator of interaction and feedback, each leader must draw heavily on his or her individual counseling skills. Verbal responses that are effective when working in a one-to-one relationship also may be effective when working in the complex of a group relationship. Various modes of response, both verbal and nonverbal, that might be helpful to a group leader are described in the following paragraphs:

Reflective Listening

Reviewing the discussion of "levels of interaction in Chapter 4 will remind the reader of a fundamental group leader function — reflective listening (levels 3-4-5).

Reflecting Content

Much of the discussion that takes place in group interaction should have a focus if members are to become aware of meanings and implications. The leader can reflect content, rephrasing material in fresh, new words, capturing the essence of the statements so that members can hear more accurately their own words and the verbalizations of others.

Avis: You might not show it right out. You may think you despise your parents and might tell everybody you hate them, but deep down you actually know you really love your parents. Kids under 18 have to have someone over them, and they actually are afraid of losing that, but they don't really know it.

Leader: . . . Afraid of losing the security of having someone responsible for you.

Avis: Yes, all kids need someone to tell them what to do.

Leader: It sounds like you're saying, Avis, that you appreciate having someone older help you make decisions at times.

Reflecting Feelings

Anyone trained in a nondirective stance is adept at reflecting feelings. The response is difficult to learn, but once learned, becomes almost automatic. The danger of this verbal response pattern is that it can become trite and parrot-like, and therefore insulting. A group leader must be sensitive in order to verbalize feelings accurately and should be careful not to mind-rape in the process.

Greg: I really don't want to lose Shirley, but I simply don't know what I can do to prevent it from happening.

Leader: . . . and that's a pretty helpless feeling.

Greg: That's it — helpless. I'd be willing to do almost anything to keep her interested in a close relationship. But then, sometimes I get the feeling that it all has been pretty one-sided, with *me* making all the effort.

Leader: It's like a double bind for you. You want Shirley badly but not at the price of losing your self-respect.

Linking

The process of tying one member's comments to another member's comments may be helpful at times. The linking response may involve either ideas or feelings, and perhaps may link verbal and nonverbal messages.

> *Jeanne:* The pressures of going to school, working, and trying to live a healthy, balanced life are overwhelming me.

> *Leader:* That seems to have become a recurring theme in our group. Can you identify with anyone else in our group who might be experiencing your feelings?

or

> *Leader:* The way you abruptly sat up, Harry, gives me a hunch that Jeanne struck a responsive chord with you.

Speaking Congruently ("I" Messages)

Congruent speaking is another important communicating skill. Reflective listening alone is insufficient for enhancing communication between people. A world of listeners would be a quiet place indeed.

One of the goals of a group leader is to help members reduce their possible inhibitions about self-disclosure. Telling another person exactly what is on your mind at all times is not what is being proposed here. Sometimes, cruelty has been passed off as "being honest" or "telling it like it is." An extensional group is an appropriate environment for self-disclosing and providing feedback to others in the form of congruent messages. The "onion" model of self-disclosure in Chapter 1 provides a framework for fully understanding the notion of congruent messages. In a congruent message the speaker expresses his or her internal feelings and perceptions as truly and as completely as possible while he or she is experiencing them. This is a message in which observable behavior and verbal reports match up.

110

A common tendency is to suppress or conceal feelings, to make less than a complete report of what is happening within us. We tend to label other persons instead of expressing feelings and perceptions and assuming responsibility for them. When someone says, "You're neat!" it probably means, "I feel good when I'm with you." "You're evasive" (a label) could really mean, "I'm frustrated by my lack of success in making contact with you.'

Congruent messages, then, are attempts to speak authentically in the here and now. Risks are involved. The person to whom you are attempting to be congruent may not accept what you are saying. To have our good intentions misinterpreted does not feel good. On the other hand, withholding a congruent message to avoid risk does nothing to enhance meaningful communication and interaction. The group leader must model congruent speaking and be alert to recognize when it is happening with group members. The skill of congruent speaking is important to the group process, particularly when confrontation is involved.

Perception Checking

Perception checking is an attempt to see if another person's feelings are as you think they are. This is certainly important for group leaders in terms of confirming their intuition and in modeling appropriate group behavior for members. Perceptions are influenced by what is said and observed. Group members must have opportunities to express their perceptions so they may be confirmed, adjusted, or rejected. Misperceptions lead to prejudices and distortions.

> *Jim:* John, you seem angry with me. You have been very quiet since I shared my feelings with you.

> *John:* No, I'm not upset. I have been thinking about what you said a few minutes ago. I need time to sort it out in my mind.

111

Had Jim not checked his perception with John, the misperception may have remained an interference between them. The chances of their establishing an open, caring relationship would most likely have been decreased.

Feelings were intense as June revealed her feelings about a possible separation from her husband. As she began to cry softly, Pat, who had been listening intently, also began to cry. With tears streaming down her cheeks, she grinned and said, "This is silly!"

Ed said, "I'm confused, Pat. What's silly? I can't tell if you're happy or upset."

Pat replied angrily, "I'm upset! Any fool can see that."

The leader intervened. "I think Ed's confusion is shared by others, Pat. I'm having difficulty understanding also." Several heads nodded confirmation. "Please, can you help us? You're obviously crying, but you looked as if you were laughing, too."

Pat explained that she had identified closely with June because she was recalling the time when she divorced her first husband several years previously. When she could not contain her tears in recalling an event that should have been long forgotten, she thought of herself as being foolish. At this point she was chastising herself with, "This is silly!" — "this" meaning her tears.

The leader's attempt to understand Pat's situation was an example of perception checking. He was sharing his observation of what seemed to be Pat's feelings, and asked for clarification. Ed's report of his feelings (confused) was an attempt to check his perception. Perception checking requires the courage to risk being misunderstood or misinterpreted. It is an invitation to share and confirm experiences. Although it is not limited to confrontation, perception checking is obviously a vital part of implementing confrontation as a startegy. And the value of checking positive perceptions should not be overlooked. They are as important to facilitating the group process as are negative perceptions.

The Eyes of the Leaders

Observing nonverbal behavior provides valuable information for sharpening communication and group interaction (Chapter 6 contains more about nonverbal awareness). It has been said that we "tend to believe our eyes more than our ears"; that is, if we perceive incongruity in what we see and what we hear, we are likely to believe what we see. It is like the Don Knotts comedy bit. Bug-eyed and visibly shaking, he is asked, "Are you nervous?" In a quivering, squeaky voice, he quickly replies, "Nope!" as he continues to shake. The visible behavior seems more significant than his denial.

One caution is crucially important when using nonverbal cues in communication. This is rooted in the authors' existential philosophy that each person is ultimately responsible for himself or herself. One can speak only for oneself. This view conflicts with some of the popular literature on nonverbal communication (Fast, 1971; McGough, 1974) that associates universal meanings with certain nonverbal behaviors. For example, locked thumbs in the belt directly above the pockets supposedly indicate male sexual availability; arms folded tightly across the chest are supposed to mean "closed to discussion." But it is possible that the man with thumbs in his belt does not know what to do with his hands and that the person with folded arms is cold. The advertising blurb for one popular book on nonverbal communication promises that you can "penetrate the personal secrets, both of intimates and total strangers" if you read the book (Fast, 1971). Even if it were possible to use nonverbal information to "penetrate" someone's inner life-space, such a practice would be unethical and would ruin communication rather than enhance it.

Research has demonstrated that, in fact, some nonverbal cues are universal — e.g, pupils of the eyes dilate when we feel loving and they contract when we feel hateful (Hess, 1975). Sophisticated procedures (pupillometrics) and research acumen are required to make sense out of such nonverbal cues.

113

A more practical application of nonverbal communication is to trust one's intuition as to what the cues are suggesting (Sielski, 1979). The key is for observers to share what they are perceiving and to accept responsibility for having interpreted the cues as they have. Responsibility for the meaning of non-verbal cues remains with the observer, not the behaver, Risks are involved in offering a perception of another person's nonverbal behavior, just as they are in confrontation and perception checking. Recipients are free to do as they choose with the information. They can accept it, reject it, ignore it, qualify it, justify it, and so on. Recipients are responsible for determining what value perceivers' information is to them.

The Ears of the Leaders

The *eyes* of the leaders constantly monitor nonverbal com-munications within the group; the *ears* of the leaders constantly monitor verbal communications. This listening and hearing constitute the listening skills of leaders. They see, hear, feel, sort, discriminate, react, act. The ears of the leaders are antennae that pick up not only surface content, but also meanings and implications that are not always apparent to the untrained listener. The listening-responding feedback role of group leaders *must* be based on a thorough working knowledge of personality theory. Background in the dynamics of human behavior must be a part of the professional preparation leaders bring to groups. The following comments, it is hoped, will help identify possible areas of sensitive listening that might be processed by group leaders as they function as facilitators. We do not intend to provide a "listening cookbook" that can substitute for extensive background in psychological theory.

One major "listening post" for leaders who function in the extensional model is the explicit and implicit value hierarchies of each member. Participants can extend their life-spaces more effectively if they are aware of the value bases from which they operate. Leaders can use their listening skills to help members "hear" their value systems (Blaker, in press). As members inter-act, these systems are clearly disclosed and, when appropriate,

114

leaders can provide feedback. Obviously, leaders avoid judgmental responses. The "goodness" or "badness" label attached to a value arises from a member. Leaders neither approve nor disapprove. Their task is to help members each "hear" their own values and become aware of their priorities. What an individual member does with this knowledge outside the group is his or her responsibility.

Adult participants, through their verbal and nonverbal expressions, indicate that they have internalized stances toward the traditional cultural values of work, achievement, "things," friends, cleanliness, honesty, learning, thrift, travel, and so forth, but they may be only dimly aware of how these stances have been translated into a unique life-style. Pre-adolescent and adolescent participants, through verbal and nonverbal expressions, may reveal their questioning of traditional cultural value systems. As they examine their own values, however, they may find that they are chiefly "reactive" rather than "proactive" — i.e., *against* something rather than *for* something. The value of nonconformity, for example, requires a conformity against conforming, or a conformity of nonconforming. Group leaders use *their* listening skills to help participants identify their existent value systems and become aware of the accompanying implications for life-styles.

Leaders listen, too, to life-space verbalizations about things members may wish to change. For instance, leaders may take particular note of expressions of inadequacy, incompetency, worthlessness, despair, expressions of "I'm not okay," and so on. These negative self-expressions probably represent elements participants would like to change in their personality functioning. Comments about feelings of rejection, whether it be of others or oneself, of wishes to "get even" or to be punished — in general, of deficiency needs — may point to areas members want to examine. Verbalizations of guilt feelings, feelings of loneliness, of isolation, or depression may indicate a "human nourishment" deficiency, and perhaps in group this deficiency could be relieved.

Again, leaders may or may not respond verbally to the content they "hear." They may only make mental notes of overt or covert expressions of a member's ambivalent, conflicted

115

feelings about a significant other. A leader may only silently monitor expressions of members' neurotic needs to control and manipulate others. In the extensional model leaders are more likely to respond verbally to non-neurotic needs of creativity, self-expression, and enjoyment. In general, in this model leaders process both deficiency and growth needs, but they may respond verbally more frequently to the latter.

A thorough knowledge of defense mechanisms is essential for group leaders. Rationalizations, projections, intellectualizations, denials, and so forth may be data that a leader might process but not verbalize. The current developmental task that each member is addressing, however, probably will be identified to bring it into the member's awareness so that he or she can more actively cope with it.

The ears of the leader are acutely tuned to grammatical and speech-pattern cues to understanding a member's frame of reference. If a leader is to be of use to members in extending their functioning, the leader must understand that frame of reference. One way to do this is to pick up speech cues.

In the writers' experience, any statement beginning with "I" is important. "My," "mine," "ours," should be distinguished if the speaker's frame of reference is one of undue possessiveness or of being self-responsible. "Shoulds" and "oughts" are significant other-directed speech patterns. Any statement qualified by "but," any statement seeking approval (such as "okay?" at the end of a statement), excessive verbiage, excessive questioning, sighs, excessive explainings, apologies, speech intonations and hesitancies, demanding, commanding, doubting, contradicting — all represent verbal cues that a leader processes so that he or she can enter fully into the life-space of a member. The intent is not to violate life-space but to use professional skills to extend a member's life-space.

Communication Patterns to Avoid

Certain speech behaviors are not helpful in communication in group. Questioning has already been discussed as basically hostile and as a way of controlling others. Interpreting can be a form of mind-raping, which is avoided in the extensional model. Calling attention to the group process is not helpful, because it tends to make an object out of the group and thus of group members. The authors suggest that leaders avoid talking about the process itself with the group except when training leaders. Summarizing is seldom helpful. This speech pattern "places a period on communication," which may inhibit growth. Instead of summarizing, group leaders might routinely "cap" at the end of each session (see Chapter 4). Speech patterns of "I hear you saying . . ." are irritating and often represent mind-raping. Sentences beginning with, "You feel . . .," "You are feeling . . ." can be patronizing, and they also may represent mind-raping. Any efforts to elicit a "because" answer or an answer to a "why" are not helpful.

"Should" and "should not," "don't worry," "I was there, too," "I understand how you feel because . . .," "I coped with it, so you can" are all speech patterns that must be avoided by group leaders. Members may exhibit these verbal behaviors, but leaders should not. Straight comments, clear positions, risk of self, and I-to-Thou verbalizations are helpful. When leaders function as communication facilitators, they model these speech patterns.

SUMMARY

The four micro-functions of group leadership have been addressed in this chapter: traffic-directing, modeling, being an interaction catalyst, and facilitating communication. As was pointed out in the introductory remarks, sometimes these functions overlap and interweave, and sometimes they are discrete. The four functions are observable to some degree in all interaction groups, even if the group leader's theoretical stance may be something other than extensional. Although the purposes and settings of groups vary (e.g., school versus senior citizens' group), the four leader functions are roughly the same in an extensional model. All group leaders perform some type of

117

traffic-directing; all group leaders model in some fashion; all group leaders use some type of catalyst for stimulating inter-action; all group leaders facilitate communication in various ways. A group leader who performs the four functions with reasonable skill and self-assurance should expect a productive group outcome.

REFERENCES

Blaker, Kenneth E. "Counseling and Values," in Brian P. Hall and Larry Rosen (Eds.), *Readings in Values and Meaning.* New York: Paulist Press, in press.

Carkhuff, Robert R., and Berenson, Bernard G. *Beyond Counseling and Therapy.* New York: Holt, Rinehart, and Winston, 1967.

Dreyfus, Edward A. "Humanness: A Therapeutic Variable," *Personnel and Guidance Journal,* (February 1967), pp. 48-56.

Fast, Julius. *Body Language.* New York: Pocket Books, 1971.

Harris, Thomas. *I'm Okay, You're Okay.* New York: Harper & Row, 1969.

Hess, Eckhard H. *The Tell-Tale Eye: How Your Eyes Reveal Hidden Thoughts and Emotions.* New York: Van Nostrand Reinhold Co., 1975.

McGough, Elizabeth. *Understanding Body Talk.* New York: Scholastic Book Services, 1974.

Passons, William R. *Gestalt Approaches in Counseling.* New York: Holt, Rinehart, and Winston, 1975.

Sielski, Lester M. "Understanding Body Language," *Personnel and Guidance Journal,* January 1979, pp. 238-242.

6

Using Nonverbal Information

6

Using Nonverbal Information

A group leader's alertness and sensitivity to nonverbal data can provide a rich source of interactive material, both in terms of using nonverbal catalysts to stimulate interaction, and of noticing and using nonverbal cues to help members clarify themselves.

In a group of graduate students, a young woman's aloof attitude toward the group was causing several members to have negative feelings about her. As the group progressed over several sessions, one member finally found the courage to share his feelings with her. As he talked about his negative feelings, the young lady crossed her right leg over her left knee and locked her ankles together tightly. Her arms were folded severely across her chest, and her breathing increased noticeably.

When asked if she felt tense after hearing negative things being said to her, she replied cooly, "No, not at all. I'm perfectly calm." Upon hearing this, another group member confronted her with a description of what he was perceiving. He described her tight posture, heavy breathing, and his impression of how she could understandably be "uptight" at having someone unload negative feelings on her.

As she listened to the group members' perceptions, she began to relax and finally shared in a quivering voice that she had been petrified with fear about being in a group. She was consciously attempting to avoid any kind of interaction with others. What had appeared to the group to be aloofness was really an attempt to protect herself from unknown fears. Her authentic disclosures to the group, prompted by the confrontation, completely changed the nature of the group's interaction. Negative feelings changed to caring and supportive feelings, and she became more secure and relaxed.

The thumb tucked tightly inside a fist, a flexing jaw muscle, arms folded tightly across the chest, the drumming of an index finger, the selection of a floor cushion as a seat — these all represent important messages to group leaders. Although leaders may not always respond immediately or verbally to these silent signals, they observe and draw tentative meaning from them. When verbal and nonverbal cues seem incongruent, when the tone of voice says one thing while the words say another, when lips are smiling but hands are clenched, the leader's vigilance system is called into play. The language of nonverbal communications in group is rich with silent signals that can be received by a leader's sensitive antennae. The leader "hears" as many of these signals as possible, then responds selectively and in a self-responsible manner.

Research evidence indicates that specific nonverbal behaviors may have specific psychological meaning (Mahl, 1968; Mehrabian, 1971; Ekman & Friesen, 1975; Beier, 1966). For the present, such evidence must be viewed as tentative; nevertheless, Mahl's 1968 study of gestures and body movements seems most relevant. He suggested that certain specific acts seemed to express the same kinds of feelings in all of his subjects. For example, making a fist, rubbing one's nose, shrugging the shoulders, interest in fingernails, and interest in teeth generally indicate hostility. Scratching, for example, is considered by some as hostility turned inward. A person who sits rigidly erect with hands folded in the lap is seen as exerting tight control over hostile and aggressive impulses. The frequency of foot movements and general postural shifts provides a good estimate of anxiety. These are merely suggestions, of course — not indisputable facts.

122

Mehrabian (1971) reported that posture may indicate degree of liking and status. The more someone leans toward the person he or she is speaking to, the more positive is the feeling about that person. Direct eye contact also may be an indication of positive regard and, conversely, habitual avoidance of eye contact may be an expression of fear or dislike. By the way, Mehrabian's research estimates that as much as 60 percent of a verbal message's meaning is transmitted through body movement, positioning, and posture.

The foregoing findings must be viewed as tentative, because other writers have indicated that nonverbal messages do not have universal meanings (Hall, 1959). But group leaders need not be tentative about increasing their awareness of nonverbal group behavior, however tentative their interpretation of the silent signals may be. They should be alert to changes of posture and relaxation and tensing of muscles. They can note changes in rates of speech, direction of gaze, length of messages and silences, changes in facial expressions, and members' postures. Some of the nonverbal behaviors that seem important to us are described below; you will no doubt want to lengthen the list.

But first an important issue should be addressed: What can group leaders do once they have noted a specific nonverbal behavioral response in a group member? There are at least three alternatives. One is for leaders to offer their perceptions and feelings concerning the behavior in question. For example, if a member answers a question "yes" while at the same time shaking his or her head "no," the leader may feel confused by this contradictory set of responses and let the member know it. As stated in Chapter 5, one must remember that a perception of nonverbal behavior given by the leader or any group member is the personal feeling of the individual holding the view, and the person producing the behavior may choose to accept or reject such views.

A second possibility is trying to help members express themselves by exaggerating nonverbal behavior. Frequently, group members complain that they can't feel trust, love, caring for another, aggressive feelings, or a sense of who they are. Such a member may express a lack of feeling and indicate to the group leader and members that he or she wants to experience these feelings. Often, the leader and members may have already noticed nonverbal behavior hinting at the presence of these supposedly nonexisting feelings. For example, if the member claims he or she can't feel angry, yet is perpetually frowning, the leader may suggest that the member try exaggerating this frown and include with the exaggeration any other nonverbal (or verbal) behavior that tends to arise. Amplifying or exaggerating an attitude or behavior is a potent means by which the individual can become aware of feelings that for some reason remain below the person's present level of awareness.

A host of nonverbal techniques to help people "get into their feelings" can be used by the skillful group leader. Group leaders learn through experience when the time is ripe for an exercise that might help a member break through into a new compartment of feeling self. Leaders must be cautious in using these exercises lest they force a member to become defensive and, therefore, less likely to experience his or her own feelings.

The third possibility is the one leaders use most frequently. They simply note the behavior silently, storing it away as tentative information about the group member, using this added knowledge to make better judgments as they proceed with the group process.

Frequently group members are not aware of the nonverbal messages they are sending, and the question arises whether the leaders are indulging in psychological voyeurism when they observe and try to understand meanings behind their observations. Perhaps the most honest way to handle this dilemma is for the leaders to comment in their introductory remarks that they will be attempting to communicate at all levels throughout the group process, and this includes nonverbal cues. At this point, the leaders might ask group members to react to their nonverbal behaviors and try to articulate their responses to these cues.

When a leader first chooses to react verbally to a nonverbal cue, members become self-conscious and uncomfortable, and thus feelings should be discussed openly. Once members understand that nonverbal language is only an extension of verbal language, they can come to terms with the fact that they are transmitting messages constantly, consciously or unconsciously, and that these messages are being received constantly, consciously or unconsciously.

The following comments describe silent signals sent through a person's nonverbal body language and silent signals sent in relation to others. The "Body Language" section discusses messages transmitted through posture, face, hands and feet. Nonverbal communications sent in relation to others have been subsumed under "Territoriality." The focus is on increasing the observational skills of group leaders so as to enhance their facilitating function. The various nonverbal techniques that follow might be used to help group members become more sensitive to their own and others' silent signals. Leaders must exercise judgment in introducing nonverbal catalysts into the group process. Obviously, they should have a specific purpose in mind for any given exercise. Sometimes the purpose may suggest that the entire group be involved; other times an exercise should be used only to clarify a relationship between two members. A note of caution to the leaders: The translation of silent signals is as much an art as a science; thus, the following suggestions for interpretation must invariably be weighed against the contents of the conative universe of the person reacting to the message.

BODY LANGUAGE

Body language may be "spoken" by the body as a whole or by various parts of the body. Several messages may be sent simultaneously, and at times these messages may contradict each other. A signal sent by one person may mean something entirely different when sent by another. Thus, the meaning that might be attached to a nonverbal cue depends on the sender, on the situation, and on the perceptiveness of the receiver. Common nonverbal cues can be interpreted only on the basis of a tentative hypothesis that a group leader might have about silent signals sent by group members through their body language. This language will be differentiated here by three areas: hands and feet, face, and posture.

Hands and Feet

The thumb tightly enclosed within the fist may suggest to group leaders to proceed with caution. A member who tucks both thumbs within his or her fists sends an even stronger "red flag" message. Hands held palms up may be evidence of a nondefensive stance that suggests a willingness to receive messages. Hands obscuring the mouth may indicate a desire to communicate coupled with hesitancy in doing so. Hands folded with fingers interlaced, palms loose and out, might suggest willingness to interact but with reservations, while the same hand position with fingers tightly folded and the mounts of the thumbs pressed firmly together may indicate a higher degree of defensiveness. Twirling a ring or fingering jewelry may be symptomatic of inner tensions. Cracking of knuckles suggests aggression, as well as tension and rigidity.

All of these observations are *possible* cues to inner behaviors, but, in any case, for group leaders who must be alert to all cues, verbal and nonverbal, hands are a rich source of data. Twisting of hands, hands that shake, wet hands, cold hands, clenched hands, open hands, outward-reaching hands, inward-pointing hands, the shaken finger, the raised fist, index fingers across pursed lips — all may contain messages of possible importance to the group leader.

Feet also send messages. These messages may be more easily missed than messages sent by the hands. Group leaders, therefore, should make it a point to scan the group for feet that are tapping or moving in a rhythmic manner. The message sent is probably one of inner tension. The tension may mean that the member is attending to the group intently — or it may mean that the member would like to escape from the current interchange.

Crossing the feet may mean that a member is closing off open communication, warding off threats, rejecting the group as a whole, rejecting a particular member, or it may have any number of other interpretations. Feet stretched out into a group are probably sending a different message from feet tucked up under a body or feet slid back under a chair. Taking shoes off usually signals relaxation, while feet slipping in and out of shoes may indicate ambivalence about what is happening in the group. Tracing a figure eight or a circle with a toe may indicate involvement in the group on the part of the member who is emitting this signal. The way one leg is arranged in relation to the other when standing often suggests messages. Shifts in body stances also represent messages.

Obviously group leaders cannot take in all nonverbal cues, and they most certainly cannot read them accurately all the time, but with practice and attention, a surprising number can be processed. Cues presented by the hands and feet, of course, should be considered in the context of all other nonverbal and verbal cues.

The Face

Group leaders can improve their effectiveness by learning to process the complex yet fleeting messages that the face expresses. These messages are sent by all people, whether they are speaking, listening, or withdrawn. Expressions have many connotations, ranging from boredom and daydreaming to excitement and growth.

Eyes

Of all facial features, the eyes probably send the most accurate messages (Ekman & Friesen, 1975). Although the volume of messages from the eyes is beyond what one person can handle, group leaders should process what they can as accurately as possible. Closed eyes may indicate a temporary flight —into self or away from the group. Absence of eye contact may signal a retreat to an "I-It" relationship; certainly the nonverbal message involves some loss of "I-Thou" communication.

Members who appear to be unwilling to sustain eye contact may prefer to relate to people as objects and probably tend to intellectualize as a characteristic defense mechanism. These people often can be observed shifting from a momentary eye-to-eye connection with another group member to "seeing" into space behind the addressed member, where they disconnect from others and "look at" an idea or into themselves. Once they have done this, they are essentially talking to themselves and have phased out any relationship with another. The eye contact circuit breaks, and the human connection seems to lose power. On the other hand, members who constantly look to the group leader probably are seeking approval and may need to explore dependency patterns.

Members who glare with widened eyes are hard to misunderstand. Eyes drifting out of the group speak rather loudly. Eyes glancing covertly at watches suggest a meaning that is almost unmistakable. Rapid eye movements may suggest a search for an exit. Rapid eye-blinking sometimes indicates intense disagreement or strong emotional reactions.

Another facet of eye movement worth mentioning has been presented by Cameron-Bandler (1978). An important component of her counseling theory is the concept that eye fixation (pause in eye movement), whether it be for a fleeting moment or a long pause, is a reliable indicator of visual, auditory, or kinesthetically-oriented thought.

As an exercise demonstrating this idea, ask someone a question that requires him or her to process information mentally — e.g., "What is the square root of 144?" If the person's eyes move upward, he or she is probably visualizing the square root process. If the eyes move down and to the left, the person is probably carrying on an internal dialogue (covertly talking to oneself). A kinesthetically-oriented person's eyes drop down to the right as he or she mentally writes out the numbers while thinking through the square root process. Kinesthetic people like to *do* what they are thinking about. Those who are auditory prefer to *hear* what they are thinking about. Visually-oriented people like to *see* what they are thinking about. As in the description of Jungian typology in Chapter 3, we are predominantly, not exclusively, one type. Thus, we possess all three thinking modalities and eye fixations. The preferred modality is revealed by a predominance of one type of eye fixation over the others.

How can this simple eye observation be helpful in developing group leadership skills? Chapter 8 presents several kinds of catalysts designed to stimulate group interaction. Visual members (eyes up) are believed to be most responsive to imagery and fantasy activities. Auditory members prefer talking-listening activities. Kinesthetic members appreciate activities most when they are physically involved in doing something.

All three modalities are found in most groups and, as the saying goes, "you can't please all of the people all of the time." But leaders who are interested in stimulating interaction for an individual member can choose the most appropriate activity after observing the eye movement of that member. As is true of any nonverbal cue, the success of implementing Cameron-Bandler's idea depends upon the leader's alertness, willingness to experiment, disclose his or her perceptions and feelings of the moment, and, most of all, accept recipients' right to do anything they wish with the observations the leader has provided.

The topic of eye fixation as a nonverbal cue can be explored and expanded upon as a counseling technique by reading Cameron-Bandler (1978), Bandler and Grinder (1979), and Goleman (1979).

Mouth and Voice

Nonverbal expression related to the mouth and voice offers another rich set of behavioral patterns to the attentive eyes and ears of group leaders. The smile that is not in harmony with a verbal message is usually quite apparent, as is the self-abnegating laugh, the nervous giggle, or the clearing of the throat. Group members' voices can either lack impact — hollow, droning, meek, submissive, tentative — or they can be rich, mellow, and commanding. A voice can be a little boy's or a little girl's voice, or the voice of Mother or Father. Each person's voice sends a message about the sender that is usually unconscious. Group leaders can bring part of the quality of a member's voice to their awareness.

Nonverbal messages cannot be read with certainty. To suggest that they can is irresponsible, but to ignore them is equally irresponsible. Group leaders must attempt to observe as many of these signals as possible, but they need not respond to them verbally. The majority of silent signals are processed silently by group leaders until they feel that a verbal recognition may be helpful.

Body Posture

Another source of nonverbal data is body posture. A torso leaning into a group; a torso held rigidly upright; a slumped, relaxed torso — all send quite different messages. Deep sighs, rapid breathing, a rising flush, holding the head in the hands, chewing on nails, changes of head and neck postures, changes in overall body postures, shaking a finger or a pencil authoritatively, doodling, the subtle pushing back of chairs, removing of coats, loosening of ties, clicking of nails, chewing on glasses, taking glasses on and off — all are silent signals constantly being sent throughout a group when members are settled into session.

Eric Berne's (1961) analysis of body posture from the theoretical framework of transactional analysis contains material that group leaders should find helpful. Berne suggests that body stance communicates information concerning which of the three ego states (parent, child, or adult) is in control at any given time. For example, an index finger shaking at the group suggests that the member is "coming on" in a parent ego state, while a slumped shoulder posture may indicate a child ego state. Group leaders who familiarize themselves with Berne's work will find body posture a rich source of data about members' inner worlds.

Posture messages are sent in many ways. For instance, a drastic change in mode of dress may indicate a member's change of attitude toward the group; it also may indicate a change of general group climate. Alert leaders observe which members arrive together and which members leave together. Do individual members exhibit separation anxieties when the group session ends? These anxieties are almost always sent nonverbally, and responsible leaders are sensitive to them.

TERRITORIALITY

"Territoriality" sounds like a term Konrad Lorenz would use to describe animal behavior. In fact, humans do tend to react to the physical proximity of another person. They may not *always* move to or from something overtly to adapt to their attraction or discomfort, but a host of nonverbal cues emerge when personal space becomes an individual issue. Several authors (Bakker & Bakker-Rabdau, 1973; Sommer, 1969; Hall, 1959) have suggested that we have space tolerances that are defined loosely as intimate (actual touching), personal (about 18 inches between parties), and public (more than 18 inches).

These physical distances are analogous to the self-disclosure model in Chapter 1. As we become more willing to self-disclose to another, we are more likely to feel comfortable having the other person closer to us. Our space needs and intrusion tolerances are analogous to the FIRO concept presented in Chapter 3 in that individuals have differing needs to have people near them physically. A person who is high in affection needs is likely to be a "toucher," and a person who is low in those needs maintains physical distance from others.

The amount of life-space group members unconsciously declare to be their territory may be observed by noting whether members move their chair into the circle, shift it closer to another, or position themselves so as to have maximum space between the chair or body and others in the group. In general, the person who maintains an unusually wide physical distance between his or her life-space and that of another is also likely to be more comfortable with the same psychological distance and, in all probability, uses a great deal of psychic energy to uphold a rigid defense system.

As leaders become sensitized to territoriality signals, they may note that a group member who chooses a corner is making a different statement from that made by one who chooses to sit on the floor at the foot of the leader. They might notice how subgroups arrange themselves. Do members group themselves in relation to various age groups? In relation to sexes? Who usually brings the coffee? Who sees that cups are filled? Who

131

arrives early? Late? Who tends to miss meetings? All these non-verbal choices carry some meaning. The translation of these choices into meanings and the importance of the meanings are left to the sensitivity of the leader, who has to be aware of his or her own biases and limitations, which inevitably distort input. Because of these distortions, all interpretations of these choices must remain tentative.

Nevertheless, a leader should observe territoriality statements because they provide information helpful in determining areas to explore and areas to avoid. A member who enters the group and scans the "territory" to locate competition or to locate support is more vigilant and, therefore, probably more defensive than the member who enters the group and immediately makes some sort of nonverbal contact with all other members. A member who establishes his or her territory near the door may be perceiving the group quite differently than does a member who finds the corner more comfortable. Leaders should take in as many of these signals as they can, even though they must await validation from other behaviors, both verbal and nonverbal.

SUMMARY

Group leaders who note incongruities between a member's verbal and nonverbal responses may offer their perceptions of these reponses to the member. Behavior can also be exaggerated (at the leader's direction) in order to intensity the feelings that may be associated with it. A third way in which leaders can use nonverbal information is to simply observe it and mentally record the hunch to expand their images of members. Nonverbal information that has been "tucked away" may be useful later as the member's needs and character unfold.

Competent group leaders resist the folly of interpreting nonverbal data as if there were universal and permanent meanings for everyone. The measure of leaders' skill in this area is not how accurate they are with their perceptions and interpretations, but how they use their observations in a tentative, caring, and inviting manner. Accuracy of interpreting nonverbal data is a distant second to the primacy of demonstrating interest and concern in the member.

REFERENCES

Bakker, Cornelis, and Bakker-Rabdau, Marianne. *No Trespassing! Explorations in Human Territoriality.* San Francisco: Chandler and Sharp, 1973.

Bandler, Richard, and Grinder, John. *Frogs into Princes.* Moab, UT: Real People Press, 1979.

Beier, E. *The Silent Language of Psychotherapy.* Chicago: Aldine Publishing Co., 1966.

Berne, Eric. *Transactional Analysis.* New York: Grove Press, 1961.

Cameron-Bandler, Leslie. *They Lived Happily Ever After: Methods of Achieving Happy Endings in Coupling.* Cupertino, CA: Meta Publications, 1978.

Ekman, Paul, and Friesan, Wallace V. *Unmasking the Face.* Englewood Cliffs, NJ: Prentice-Hall, 1975.

Goleman, Daniel, "People Who Read People," *Psychology Today,* Vol. 13, No. 2 (July 1979), p. 66.

Hall, Edward T. *The Hidden Dimension.* Garden City, NY: Anchor Books, 1959.

Mahl, G. "Gestures and Body Movements in Interviews," *Research in Psychotherapy.* Washington, DC: American Psychological Association, 1968.

Mehrabian, Albert. *Silent Messages.* Belmont, CA: Wadsworth Publishing Co., 1971.

Rosenfeld, Lawrence B., and Plax, Timothy G. "Clothing as Communication," *Journal of Communication,* Vol. 27, 1977, pp. 24-31.

Sommer, Robert. *Personal Space: The Behavioral Basis of Design.* Englewood Cliffs, NJ: Prentice-Hall, 1969.

_____. *Tight Spaces,* Englewood Cliffs, NJ: Prentice-Hall, 1978.

7

"Problem" Group Members

- Difficulty in Expressing Feelings
- Specific "Problem" Members
    - P.F. (Past-Future) Frances: The Member Who Cannot Talk in the Here and Now
    - Silent Sue: The Member Who Waits for Others to Speak First
    - Gregory Gabber: The Compulsive Talker
    - Denny Dependent: The Uncertain Member
    - Sam Scapegoat: The Attacked Member
    - Ursula Underdog: By Choice or By Accident, the Member Who Is Guaranteed Attention
    - Charley Challenger: The Hostile (to Authority) Member
    - Gary Garbage Dumper: The Sly, Vicious Member
    - Morose Mille: The Nothing-Ever-Goes-Right Member
    - Abbott Yeah-But: The Nothing-Will-Work Member
    - Otis Outsider: By Choice or By Accident, the Member Who Avoids Attention
- Summary

7

"Problem" Group Members

A leader can use certain strategies to influence group progress toward productive directions in spite of detraction and disruption. Disruptive or detracting (*disruptive* is intentional sabotage; *detracting* is unintentional) member behavior should not be a pervasive concern for a leader, but he or she can attempt some things without assuming an authoritarian position of chastising or demeaning the offending member. Trotzer (1977) and Shulman (1979) have recently directed attention to coping with "problem" members in a firm but gentle manner.

Regardless of the setting or the group's purpose, most members of extensional groups are present because they want to be. The extensional group model can be used effectively in some nonvoluntary group situations (discussed in Chapter 10), but for the moment we shall concentrate on voluntary groups. It stands to reason that if the group's participants are present by choice, the leader's task should be relatively easy. Unfortunately, such is not always the case. Interpersonal needs (see FIRO, Chapter 3) are far too complex to permit simple predictions of what to expect, even from a group of voluntary participants. They offer no guarantees for a smoothly running group. Part of the leader's hard work is trying to assure that all group members are included as contributors to the group process. For the most part, members respond positively to the opportunity, but at times an individual member's resistive group behavior slows the process and inhibits others. The resistance does not have to be vocal or aggressive. Quiet withdrawal can also be a form of resistance.

The member's resistance might be against the leader, against certain fellow group members, against the group as a collective body, or against taking responsibility for self. Resistance is manifest in numerous forms, and the motivation for resistance is complex. Some members may have excessive needs for controlling others. They may fear losing self-control. Perhaps a member fears the unknown, never having experienced the kind of interpersonal contact that is encouraged in an extensional group. Or a member may simply lack interpersonal skills. Moreover, detracting members may not even be aware of their resistance.

For the most part, a leader should maintain objectivity when encountering such members. Resistive-detracting members are probably protecting themselves in some way, whatever the actual form of their behavior. If leaders are aggressive in their efforts to ameliorate the situation, this may legitimize the member's perception that he or she needs to protect the self.

Andy had not uttered a word since he joined the group. He had picked his nails, slouched in his seat, and indicated every sign of non-interest. Now, toward the close of the second session, he was leaning forward with one hand on his knee and the other gripping the edge of his chair. His tension seemed to be connected somehow with several people who had been exchanging warm, positive feelings about each other. Suddenly he exploded at the leader, "Can I be excused from this sugar sweet crap!"

The leader responded, "Sure, Andy . . . but before you go, would you tell me if there is something that I or someone else has done to offend you?" In a rapid, staccato-like voice Andy aired his resentment about sensitivity training and "groupie-types" who go around dripping sweetness and talking group jargon. As he unloaded his anger, he began to appear calmer and the tone of his voice became softer. He said that if anyone in the group would say something nice to him, he would have difficulty believing it because that's what they were *supposed* to do.

After venting his feelings, he began to explore with the group why the positive sharing had upset him so. He eventually concluded that because he had difficulty in expressing and receiving positive comments, he feared he would end up looking "stupid" because he believed he couldn't do what the other members were doing.

The extensional group model assumes that individuals are responsible for themselves. Futhermore, the model assumes that when individuals take reponsibility for themselves, their potential for personal development is maximized. When group leaders confront detracting members, perhaps sharing their negative feelings, the leaders are speaking for themselves. The members can do what they wish with the information. At the moment leaders — or anyone else for that matter — confront someone with an expectation that the person "shape up," they have violated a basic principle of the extensional group model. This may be difficult to abide by sometimes, but leaders should keep in mind that other members present in the group have thoughts and feelings about the detracting member, the leader, and the situation. Coping with a detracting member can actually be stimulating to the group process.

DIFFICULTY IN EXPRESSING FEELINGS

A common problem among detracting group members, and many of their cooperative fellow group members as well, is the difficulty some members have in expressing their feelings. How many times have we said, "I feel," when what we have represented is not a feeling at all, but a thought? For example, someone says, "I feel the Oakland A's are the best team in baseball." That is not a feeling statement; it is a thinking statement.

Feelings are intensely personal, often tentative, and once exposed, they can make us feel vulnerable. Group members have difficulty expressing feelings either because they don't want to risk expressing them or because they are unaccustomed to expressing them. Recognition and expression of feelings as they are occurring is vital if members are to benefit from the group process. Difficulties with expressing feelings pose a particular problem in extensional group situations, in which personal insights and growth depend upon honest communication of here-and-now feelings.

In the beginning group sessions it is useful to use techniques and games as catalysts for focusing on feelings. The "Color Card" game (Chapter 8) is an example of a low-threat exercise that can help reluctant members experiment with their expression of feelings. Another technique that leaders might employ is to observe the reluctant member closely, looking for nonverbal indications of feelings, and then to share their hunches about what they think the person is experiencing. The description should be couched in behavioral terms. For example, "Jerry, you are frowning; my hunch is that you don't necessarily agree with what is being said" is an invitation for Jerry to share what is going on within.

What often appears to be an unwillingness to communicate feelings may be simply an inability to identify the feelings at a particular moment. Even if we recognize existing feelings, our vocabulary often limits our ability to communicate them. Expressing feeling as metaphors is sometimes helpful: for example, "I feel alive and bouncy like a playful puppy," or, "I'm so confused I feel like I'm in a maze and can't find my way out." Another useful technique is to have members close their eyes and try to picture the feeling and then report the first impressions that come to mind.

Although the importance of expressing feelings is foremost in the group process, no one should be forced into expressing feelings. If a leader can help group members be open enough to say, "I'm feeling pressured," he or she has functioned effectively as a group leader.

SPECIFIC "PROBLEM" MEMBERS

Because the types of behavior illuminated in the following paragraphs have appeared in several of our groups and were manifested by several individuals, we have found it convenient to create our own nontechnical labels to summarize our description of their behavior. The labels are not intended to be demeaning, and they are *never* used in the group itself.

As you will see, some members are suspected to have malevolent intentions; they may tax the patience and compassion of the most skillful and dedicated group leader. The suggestions offered as corrective or helping strategies have been most consistently effective for us. The reader is reminded that no group leader or technique is guaranteed to be 100 percent effective. We admit openly that we have experienced failure at times, perhaps because we selected the wrong technique or strategy for the specific moment or specific individual. More often, we have been able to explain our failures by recognizing that we were not aware of ourselves at that particular moment.

We emphasize that leaders' self-awareness, sensitivity to others, and courage to act are far more critical in determining their success than are their abilities to accurately "categorize" individual group members and to employ the proper technique.

P. F. (Past-Future) Frances:
The Member Who Cannot Talk in the Here and Now

The most effective mode for sustained productive group interaction is that of helping group members talk in the here and now as much as possible. Although some members of groups are open and take pleasure in sharing personal anecdotes and tales in the group, this "sharing" of intimate information can lead to a common pitfall for the beginning group leader. In his or her desire to keep the group moving and get into meaningful interaction, the leader may be reinforcing nonproductive and potentially damaging behavior in the group. The problem with this kind of interaction is that some of the stories told include people not directly involved in the group. This is an invasion of privacy and does little to help members of the group interact with each other at the present moment. Even if the stories being related are about the person telling the story, they usually are centered in the past and acquire the nature of a third-person narrative.

If personal growth is to take place, the leader must help members focus on their feelings in the present. The leader can help accomplish this by listening to the story and reacting to the feelings, not to the specifics of the incident.

Imagine a student saying, "I hate Mr. Johnson. He's the worst biology teacher at this school. Do you know what he did? He refused to accept my paper because it was three days late, and that's going to be a major part of my grade. He really likes to flunk kids. He's unfair!" At this point, the leader has the option of focusing on Mr. Johnson: "Oh, you think he's really a hard-line teacher." Or, the leader could focus on the student's feelings: "You're not accustomed to being treated that way by a teacher, and it makes you feel angry and helpless."

Using this technique of focusing on feelings, the leader has determined the direction of the group. The group will either be telling stories and airing grievances about unpopular teachers or it will be dealing with feelings of failure and frustration members might be experiencing.

Silent Sue: The Member Who Waits for Others to Speak First

Groups commonly include members who wait for others to speak or to participate first, particularly in the early stages of group development. The behavior pattern of reluctant members usually falls into one of at least two categories.

The first encompasses reluctant members who, through silence, exhibit what we have interpreted to be fear or anxiety about participating in the group. They feel that if they wait to be the last to speak, the group may overlook them, or perhaps time will run out, and thus they can avoid having the focus directed toward them. Individuals who are in this category are not necessarily opposed to being in group. They probably enjoy the sense of "belonging to" and "sharing in" the experience. Consequently, they want to be a part of it, but they have an understandable anxiety about how to begin.

The leader can give these people a great deal of support. By respecting their silence, the leader allows them time to observe and become acquainted with the group process. The leader allows them to assess their own readiness to participate. Silence often stems from fear of being attacked, ignored, or rejected. Possibly silence is a means of avoiding the risk of feeling foolish or appearing dumb. The leader must be certain that a quiet member is not compromised in the group. If the member's silence is questioned by another member, and in the leader's opinion the individual is visibly disturbed, the leader should direct the interaction to the group in general, asking something like, "Has anyone else found it difficult to get started?" or, "Does participating in the group cause anxiety in anyone else?"

For many individuals who wait for others to go first, there is another common pattern of behavior, that of simply rephrasing what has already been said by someone else.

In a high school group, members were taking turns sharing their observations and insights as to why John (a group member) seemed to inspire trust and confidence from his peers. Tom, a member, repeated what another member had said previously. This had become a regular pattern for him and it had begun to concern the leader, as it was affecting Tom's progress in the group. At this moment Melinda said, "Tom, you always say what everyone else says. Don't you have a mind of your own?" Tom was obviously stunned. Not knowing how to respond, yet feeling attacked, he replied, "Maybe someone else did say it, but it *was* my feeling."

This kind of exchange can go on indefinitely if the leader or another member does not intervene. Two possible intervening strategies come to mind. One, the leader can give support to Tom by affirming his participation. The leader could say something like, "Tom, I had the same feeling about John. I'm glad you saw it too. Is there anything you can say to him that is unique from what has already been said? What do you see in John that others might not see?" In this situation the leader has reinforced Tom's participation but has also allowed for his continued and more personal involvement in the group.

143

The second strategy would be to intervene and direct the attention away from Tom and toward Melinda. Questioning can be an indirect and unfair method of having another person share his or her feelings without risking one's own. By having Melinda restate her concern for Tom's participation, the leader can direct the group to the here and now, and also have Melinda "own" her feelings rather than having Tom attempt to "own" the incorrect concept of not having a mind of his own. The leader can simply intervene and say, "You seem upset by Tom's reaction. I would like it if you would put your concerns into a statement rather than a question."

The group leader must be especially alert for opportunities to be in touch with reluctant members, although they may prefer not to be in the spotlight. Eye contact is an important nonverbal means of communicating. Without words the leader can acknowledge the shy member's presence and reaffirm the leader's acceptance and support.

Another technique that has helped quiet members gain confidence is to use reaction papers, written after each group session. This method has been employed successfully with college-age groups. Reaction papers summarize impressions and thoughts about the group experience. Quite often, reluctant members are willing to write the things they may feel inhibited about saying in the group. This gives the leader a form of self-disclosure, which usually strengthens the bond between member and leader. It also provides a low-threat means of expression. And reluctant members often say later in group what they had written earlier on the reaction paper. The paper allowed them an opportunity to formulate and "rehearse" their thoughts before expressing them verbally.

Several catalysts are helpful for bringing out reluctant participants. For example, "Pair and Share" (Chapter 8) is an effective, low-threat catalyst for helping reluctant members or shy members to become involved.

Gregory Gabber: The Compulsive Talker

The monopolizing, compulsive talker, often an individual who is among the first to speak in the initial group session, appears to be the opposite of the reluctant group member described above. In many instances, however, their motivations are identical. Reluctant talkers and compulsive talkers may both be motivated by fear about participating in group activities. It would be poor judgment indeed for us to interpret quantity of dialogue with authenticity of feelings. In fact, dominating talkers often use excessive verbiage as a smokescreen to obscure their inability or unwillingness to really interact at a feeling level. It is as if they have said to themselves, "Well, they can't get me for not participating. If it's talking they want, I'll give them plenty." These are the most likely candidates to break silences or to fill in if they experience a lull in the interaction. Compulsive talkers are frequently story tellers, incident relaters, or gossipers. They will probably reply in an incredulous manner when someone observes, "You really haven't shared much of yourself."

Members who speak first are often aware that the intensity of interaction will pick up with time, and they are anxious to "get out there fast, pay my dues, and get back home before things really get going." They have learned the delicate balance of giving the group just enough to keep them satisfied, but not enough to let anyone get too close.

Any technique that encourages feedback in a low-threat framework should be effective in helping Gregory receive other members' perceptions. Suggested catalysts in Chapter 8 are "First Impressions," the "Metaphor Game," "Speculation," and the "Adjective Game." The leader should be alert to see that the feedback is being offered constructively. The goal is not to "put down" compulsive talkers but to help them perceive themselves more realistically.

Denny Dependent: The Uncertain Member

Leaders can make some fairly accurate judgments about a member's dependency needs if they observe revealing clues. Dependent members have frequent eye contact with the leader. They may actually be talking with someone else in the group while actively looking for acknowledgment from the leader. A common indication of dependency on the leader is the member who talks to another member through the leader.

Maria had been telling the group about a recent breakup with her boyfriend. She didn't seem too upset by the situation and had probably been active in bringing it to an end. She said, shrugging, "I could get him back any time I want!" This comment brought immediate response from Linda: "Maria is so arrogant about the fact that she can snap her fingers and boys will come running. She seems so conceited." Linda was talking about Maria to the leader, as if Maria was not there. The leader urged Linda, "Can you tell that directly to Maria?"

This bit of traffic-directing — speaking directly to someone in the group — encourages members to send direct messages and does not allow them to use the leader as a buffer or filter for statements they may fear risking.

Another characteristic of dependency is the restatement or mimicking of the leader's own behavior. This is sort of a "me too" behavior. The leader says, "Don, I'm really pleased about the way you have shared yourself with us today." The dependent member is right there with "Yeah, Don, that's really neat," and then looks to the leader.

Although the leader may be the primary focus of a member's dependency, on occasions dependency may develop with other members. This behavior is similar to that of members who wait for someone else to speak first.

Some suggestions for dealing with dependent members are:

1. Be aware of dependency as it is developing. Do not reinforce it by allowing the dependent member to feed off the leader's approval. Try not to engage dependent members in eye contact when you suspect they are looking for affirmation. Be aware of subtle nods in the direction of these members that may be conveying approval.

2. Share observations and feelings about what is going on. Leaders should not only disclose their observations, but also should check with others to see if their perceptions compare. It will be revealing to the leader if they do not. Dependency *could* be an erroneous perception on the leader's part.

3. Attend to dependent members selectively, since the leader's attention seems to be reinforcing to them. Consciously look for ways to affirm indications of independent behavior, since that is a goal of increased growth and self-awareness.

Sam Scapegoat: The Attacked Member

Group "scapegoats" come in many different varieties. They may babble endlessly, ramble, tell "tales," and generally remain at the "D" (outer) level of disclosure. They may pontificate, convince, argue, preach, or cajole. They may act dumb, not "getting" what is happening, although it is clear to everyone else. They may play the devil's advocate.

Regardless of their unique style, scapegoats invariably become the focal point of negative feelings from group members. The negative feelings are generated by obvious inconsistencies between what the scapegoat says and what seems to be honest to the group.

Bill had served 26 years in the Army. Since his retirement he had been working on his master's degree in counseling. During a group session Bill began to expound on his views of "hippie long-hairs and braless babes." Several younger members of the group immediately challenged him. The discussion became heated.

Two opposing camps were forming for battle, and the leader moved to get the group to deal in the here and now rather than on issues that were outside the group. "Let's check ourselves by examining our (the students arguing) feelings right now. Try to determine what's happening inside

147

of you." Most of the combatants expressed their feelings of being "pissed," "angry and upset," "rejected," and so on. Bill announced that he had no feelings at all, although his red face, heavy breathing, and sharp, loud tone of voice suggested otherwise. His denials and inconsistencies about his feelings and behavior caused other members to become upset with him. He was becoming the target of a lot of negative feelings.

The leader's strategy of inviting perceptions and feedback about dishonest talkers should be employed cautiously. Although most group members unload on the scapegoat to vent their negative feelings toward his or her behavior, a few members may attack to prevent themselves from becoming the focus of the group.

Inexperienced group leaders often allow the focus to remain on the scapegoat, because it assures interaction. Concentrating on the scapegoat for long periods of time is unproductive and, in the scapegoated member's case, it could actually be harmful. Consequently, as negative as the reactions may be toward the scapegoat, the leader is still responsible for seeing that the scapegoat's rights as a group member are not violated. This is relatively uncomplicated if the scapegoat has unconsciously blundered into that role. Direct feedback from members, who are reminded to use congruent messages, should keep the group at a reasonable level of integrity. Also, use of the "underdog" technique (see below) is helpful in constructively refocusing attention away from the scapegoat.

Ursula Underdog: By Choice or By Accident, The Member Who is Guaranteed Attention

The underdog concept is interesting to observe. The more an individual appears to be under attack, the greater is the probability that some group members will feel sympathetic toward the attacked person. They will sympathize with the underdog's predicament even though they might not agree with what he or she is saying. Quite often the silent members are inclined to sympathize with or support the scapegoat. At least, they may be thinking something that is nonattacking but are reluctant to become a vocal minority. They may need the leader's encouragement to express their thoughts to the scapegoat.

By observing nonverbal indications of concern, such as shifting positions, tense posture, and frowns, the leader can become sensitive to members who are withholding their feelings and thoughts. A wise strategy is to always avoid ending a group session in a negative attitude. A technique the leader might employ is to ask group members to focus on how they would feel if they were in the scapegoat's place.

Leaders also should recognize the difference between members' coming to the aid of the scapegoat because he or she has actually been wronged and behavior that is more akin to supermothering or "first aid." In the "first aid" situation a member is constantly running to someone's (anyone's) defense to distribute "Band-Aids." By protecting the aggrieved person, first-aiders feel they are also protecting themselves from attack sometime in the future. After all, medics are not *supposed* to be attacked.

Charley Challenger: The Hostile (to Authority) Member

Group behavior of hostile group members is extremely varied and complex. Their challenge of the leader could be subtle, such as "suggesting" how the leader could be more effective. At the other extreme is the overtly belligerent, hostile member who directly affronts leader responsibilities and capabilities. The time frame for a challenge varies as well. It could be a brief, temporary challenge or it could be unrelenting.

The basic message we have for the leader coping with a challenger is to "stay cool." Model self-disclosure for the group, expressing here and now thoughts and feelings authentically. Resist the urge to call Charley's bluff or put him down. When experiencing such urges, talk about them rather than act on them. Try to remain objective, with the assumption that Charley is attempting to protect himself for some reason.

The following illustrations represent the two extreme types of challengers (subtle and overtly hostile). As stated earlier, there are many varieties of challengers. The common thread for all of them is their attempt to control the leader, probably because they hope to feel more secure in the group situation.

A church group of 14 young adults met weekly, seeking spiritual and personal growth. At the first session Charlene suggested that the room was too cold and sterile to be conducive to a good group experience. She recommended that the leader (the associate pastor) locate better facilities. The leader opened the idea to the group, who determined that there wasn't any place better in the church than what they had. Before the first session ended, Charlene commented that the leader might stimulate group interaction more by using an "eye contact" exercise. Several members immediately rejected that idea for themselves because they did not want to "go too far too fast." They were content with the pace of the group interaction so far.

During the second session Charlene corrected the leader's use of "we" when referring to himself. He thanked her for the reminder. She then suggested that the group pull in a bit closer. Later, when the leader was describing a communication exercise that the group might enjoy, Charlene interrupted with, "That's OK for an opening 'get acquainted' exercise. You should have done it during our first session." The leader replied, "Charlene, I am uncomfortable with our interaction. I sense that you don't like the way I'm leading the group and you'd like me to do things differently." To that she replied, "Well, I *have* taken a graduate course in group dynamics, and in practicum I led several groups."

As Charlene described her "group credentials," Mary, another member, rolled her eyes in disgust. The leader used the nonverbal cue to refocus. "I just noticed your eyes, Mary, and I'm wondering if you want to say what's going on with you." Mary commented that she had never been in groups before and then confronted Charlene: "At first I thought you

150

[Charlene] were going to be an asset by helping inexperienced people like me. Now it looks like you're determined to take over this group. I don't like that."

Let's look at another illustration, in which the challenge is more direct.

In a public school several freshman boys who had accumulated numerous discipline referral slips were invited to participate in group counseling. The purpose of the group was to let them air their "gripes" and perhaps to help them gain some insights into their developing pattern of troubles.

The leader was successful in engaging most of the boys in talk and interaction, but Charley had placed his chair outside the group and was continually kibbitzing to the point of distraction. The leader twice invited Charley to join the group, and in each instance Charley responded with a flip, negative answer. His behavior grew worse. It seemed that Charley was intent on getting the leader to lose her "cool."

Charley finally reached into his shirt pocket, which showed the clear outline of a pack of cigarettes (against school rules). With his mouth shaped in a Cheshire cat grin, he inquired, "What are you going to do to me if I light up? I'm *dying* for a cigarette." The boys froze, waiting to see who would emerge as the winner.

The leader asked the group, "Do you think Charley really needs a cigarette right now?" One group member spoke up. "Naw — Charley's just being a smart-ass." Another group member chimed in, "He just wants to see if he can get away with it." The group then moved into a discussion of defining "smart-ass" behavior and clarifying the motivations behind it. They agreed that it was fun sometimes to be a "smart-ass." Charley did not disrupt the group again, and he did not smoke a cigarette.

Keeping "cool" in the face of challengers, whether they are subtle or direct, is easy to write about. But when the challenge actually arises, the leader's heart may beat faster and the muscles

151

become tense — the leader understandably might become absorbed with coping rather than leading. At this moment the leader will most likely begin disclosing from his or her protective "D" level.

The worst thing a leader can do is to pretend that nothing is happening. The next worse thing is to try to suppress the challenger or force compliance. Resistance met with resistance begets more resistance. The toughest, but best, leader response, in our opinion, is to struggle with authentic self-disclosure. Hopefully, this will allow the leader to capitalize on the feelings generated among other group members. Feelings and thoughts evoked among observing members can be tapped to stimulate more intense levels of interaction in the group.

Gary Garbage Dumper: The Sly, Vicious Member

The "garbage dumper" is a "cheap-shot artist." An example of Gary's style would be accusing someone of being dishonest or perverted. Even if the charge is without basis, the accusation itself has a tarnishing effect. Garbage dumpers are attackers who have never understood that people are risking something of themselves when they confront another person. Confronting is a gracious act that invites interchange for correcting misperceptions, and in this act confronters make themselves vulnerable. Garbage dumpers try to hurt. Often, their attacks are disguised in some manner, perhaps through an innuendo, and sometimes closely following someone else's verbal exchange with a group member. Garbage dumpers are effective in projecting behavior on other members that is not necessarily correct, although it may be presented as fact. Following is an illustration of a garbage-dumping statement.

Rudy had been describing his childhood as one of almost constant work. His dad was a farmer with deep religious beliefs and had taught his children that work was godly. Rudy was now trying to become more spontaneous and less compelled by the work ethic.

> *Gary:*   You must have had a really warped child-hood.

[This is a projection on Gary's part that can only make Rudy feel that maybe something was or is wrong with him. Here is another example of garbage dumping.]

In the beginning moments of a newly formed group of graduate students, members were sharing their feelings of tension. One commented that it wasn't bad for him since he had been in an encounter group before.

> *Gary:*   With that experience you probably think you're better at this than the rest of us.

The garbage dumper casts aspersions, leaves negative doubts in everyone's minds, and retreats. The element that appears in all garbage dumpers is their inability or refusal to take responsibility for their feelings. The expressed message from the "dumper" implies hurt or hostility, but the other person is projected as having the problem.

Minimizing the garbage dumper's influence on the group centers primarily on the use of gestalt methods, such as asking "dumpers" to repeat their messages using the personal pronoun, to rephrase their statements as hunches, and to encourage "victims" to express their here-and-now feelings about having been "confronted."

Morose Millie: The Nothing-Ever-Goes-Right Member

Nothing goes right for Millie. She may not intend to be negative, but her attitude is toxic to group interaction. She unleashes a string of tragedies that would make the chairs weep. Her life is ruined, she is not as pretty as, not as rich as, has a worse marriage than, fewer friends than, and so on. Millie is at a loss to describe her talents or worth. She is unsure of what she can truly claim. Sadly, Millie constantly brings on that which she fears the most. She is treated by other people exactly like she treats herself. She sees nothing positive about herself and, sure enough, other people are repulsed by her negativism. Her response to this reaction: "See, I knew they didn't like me." Ironically, Millie's talent seems to be that of predicting people's attitudes toward her — truly the self-fulfilling prophet.

The Morose Millie type presents justification for interviewing members before the group begins. By having prospective members indicate what they hope to receive from the group, the leader can assess whether the group can realistically deal with the members' stated needs. Groups are certainly not a panacea, and they are not meant for everyone. A frank discussion with the prospective member about the group process and about his or her own needs may prevent needless hurt or disappointment from unfulfilled expectations.

Techniques that could serve a useful purpose for members with extremely low self-images should focus on positive characteristics. Low-risk touching exercises may add a dimension of inclusion not often encountered by the Millies of the world. Catalysts like "Blind Walk" and "Trust Fall" (see Chapter 8) have been employed successfully for improving the positiveness of interaction. Positive verbal bombardment of any kind is essential in helping these kinds of group members refocus their identities.

Abbott Yeah-But: The Nothing-Will-Work Member

The "yeah-but" group member is one of the best examples we can think of for describing approach-avoidance behavior. Yeah-but members express a desire for help and solutions, but their behavior indicates that they really don't want these things at all. Their actions imply that they might simply want attention, and they are sure to get it if they act like they really need help to work out their particular problems. Generally, others become bored with yeah-but members rather soon and feel like giving up on them. When the leader senses his or her own or another's boredom or irritation, he or she should encourage a report of these feelings. In reporting the feelings, the leader should encourage the speaker to try to focus on the behavior that seems to be connected with the bored or irritated feelings. For example: "Don, Marsha, and Sandy have all made suggestions to try to help you solve your problem, and you have rejected them all. That makes me feel like you will reject what I might offer you." Or: "You ask for help, but you never seem to listen to anyone. When they share their ideas with you, you are so quick to tell them why they won't work."

Abbott, a strong, good-looking college freshman, had sought counseling because of his lingering unhappiness. In group he disclosed his feelings of inadequacy with girls. He hadn't had a date since arriving on campus, and his infrequent contacts with girls were awkward and uncomfortable for him.

One group member suggested that Abbott ask a buddy to fix him up with a double date. The reply was, "Most of the girls that my buddies know are dogs." A male group member shared his "technique" of seeking out girls who were sitting alone in the school cafeteria. He had met "some really neat chicks" that way. Abbott's reply was, "I'd be conscious of my table manners. The thought of eating *and* talking with girls freaks me out." Another suggestion was that he join the coed study groups at the dorm. Since he was an excellent student, he could help others in an area where he was accomplished and felt secure. The group began to turn off when he responded, "Hey, I have a tough enough time taking care of myself. I'm not about to help someone beat me on a grading curve."

Members offered a few more suggestions, only to be rejected, when finally a member said in exasperation, "Abbott, I just fantasized you with a big baseball bat. Here we are tossing you ideas, trying to help you out, and what are you doing? You're smashing the hell out of them. Well I'm not giving you any more because you'll just keep knocking them away."

The leader inquired to see if others had feelings about Abbott's persistent rejection of their contributions. Indeed, everyone seemed to have given up on Abbott.

Confronting yeah-but group members with perceptions of what is happening seems to be the most effective method for working with them. In this way, feelings are released and the yeah-but person receives feedback that he or she may choose to use. Be prepared, however, for the possibility of another yeah-but response. At this point, it may be to the group's advantage to move on to other matters.

Otis Outsider: By Choice or By Accident, The Member Who Avoids Attention

"Outsiders" may withdraw physically by moving their chairs or by assuming positions that indicate separateness. One group member chose to remove himself by lying and sitting on the floor while other group members were seated in school-type desks. Outsiders can withdraw psychologically, of course, if they regard the group's interaction as irrelevant.

Defiance, fear, and boredom are among the reasons why a person chooses to be an outsider. By carefully observing the nonverbal behavior of the outsider, a group leader can develop hunches as to Otis' motivation. Is he remaining distant because it is his preference (i.e., he has low inclusion needs — FIRO)? Has he made attempts to contribute that were rejected or unrecognized? Does someone in the group have an intimidating effect on Otis? There are moments when active members may temporarily withdraw for some reason, but their interest returns. Outsiders, though, intentionally maintain their separateness from the group. Their primary strategy is to do nothing.

Assuming that Otis wants to be part of the group process, the leader must be sensitive not to force him to participate before he is ready to contribute. Two simple procedures can be used. One is to simply ask Otis if he has something he would like to offer: "What do you think, Otis?" "Do you have any reaction to Harry's comments?" and so on. Otis may refuse, or contribute little, but the invitation has been extended. A second procedure is to contact Otis at a time other than in the group to see if something is concerning him about the group that he has not had the courage to reveal in group. Again, the leader must be careful to convey the *invitation* to participate, rather than a disguised form of pressure.

An exception to these two procedures would be when the aloof member is obviously bidding for control. In the cigarette episode described earlier, Charley is an example of an outsider who was actively trying to sabotage the group. This kind of separateness is better handled through confrontation.

Any of the involvement activities in Chapter 8, like "Aligator-Elephant," "Blind Walk," "Trust Fall," "Metaphor Game," and "Pair and Share," are suitable for helping make participation easier for outsiders.

SUMMARY

"Problem" members need not be conscious or deliberate in their actions. Their behavior can detract from the group's effectiveness quite innocently. Nevertheless, if their behavior is left unattended, the group experience can be diminished for everyone. In the extensional model, such "problem" behavior is viewed generally as a defense mechanism. Detracting members are in some way attempting to protect themselves.

The leader's task is to channel the occasion to benefit the detracting member as well as the group. The leader's reaction to the detracting member is likely to be shared by others in the group and should encourage their expression. Whether the "problem" group member's behavior is intentional or innocent, the leader's responsibility is to be honest with his or her own reactions, help others express their feelings and reactions, and be considerate of the detracting member, so that everyone in the group has an opportunity to learn from the experience.

REFERENCES

Shulman, Lawrence. *The Skills of Helping Individuals and Groups.* Itasca, IL: F. E. Peacock Publishers, 1979.

Trotzer, James P. *The Counselor and The Group: Integrating Theory, Training and Practice.* Monterey, CA: Brooks/Cole Publishing Co., 1977.

8

Catalysts for Interaction: A Collection of Verbal and Nonverbal Exercises

---

- Introduction to Catalytic Activities
- Catalytic Activities
    Leader Control
    Trotzer's Model
- Interpersonal/Verbal Activities
    Low Intensity
    Medium Intensity
    High Intensity
- Interpersonal/Nonverbal Activities
    Low Intensity
    Medium Intensity
    High Intensity
- Intrapersonal/Verbal Activities
    Low Intensity
    Medium Intensity
    High Intensity
- Intrapersonal/Nonverbal Activities
    Low Intensity
- Summary

8

Catalysts for Interaction: A Collection of Verbal and Nonverbal Exercises

INTRODUCTION TO CATALYTIC ACTIVITIES

Group leaders should not expect group members to know group process skills or to have a natural sense of what to expect. Few experiences in our lives even begin to approach the group experience. The skills required to interact quickly and productively in the unique situation that is group are quite different from those that keep social interactions comfortable. In everday social intercourse, polite consideration for another's feelings is essential. Censoring feelings and reactions is necessary in most employment situations. Without basic good manners we could not live and work together in harmony. Of course, it is naive to assume that authenticity in group implies blurting out *every* "gut level" response the moment it comes to mind.

In ordinary interactions we do and must make a presentation of self that reflects only a portion of our multilevel selves —cognitive, conative, and sensual; conscious, preconscious, and unconscious — or only a portion of our many roles as worker, parent, offspring, companion, lover, friend. All of our social roles require some censoring in our presentation of self if we are to remain functional. (Note "Area of Free Activity" on Johari Window and Level "D" of the "onion model" in Chapter 1.)

Group is something else. Here, as leaders, we ask participants to forego the normal social habits that are essential

161

outside the group. We ask members to temporarily give up customary politeness, refrain from censoring, and respond to other group members with a multilevel presentation of self. We ask members to report their feelings, thoughts, and spontaneous reactions to each other freely and fully without being concerned about the usual social rules. We ask them to interact with each other at levels that would be awkward if they were maintained consistently in the world outside the group. With even the most trusting group member, these can be difficult requests. With members who are less trusting, more inhibited, or resistive, these requests can be formidable.

We have found communications exercises or activities to be a useful vehicle for making the transition from the outside world to group. They are effective in reducing reluctance and promoting a willingness to interact in a manner that we know to be vital for a growth experience. Some exercises can move participants to deeply intense emotional levels. Because of the stimulating character of these activities, we think of them as "catalysts."

The catalytic activities presented in this chapter are designed to stimulate interaction that will enable leaders to perform their leadership functions. Catalysts are *not* the most important part of a leader's arsenal of techniques, but they do provide added potential for leading creatively. They should be used sparingly and only when the group grants permission to use them. Opening every session with a catalyst or indiscriminately including an exercise during each session is questionable. Leaders who rely primarily on catalytic activities to maintain (rather than *stimulate)* interaction are certainly not skilled. On the other hand, leaders who sit back and wait for interaction are either lazy or ignorant of techniques that could increase their effectiveness.[1]

---

[1] Rogerian encounter groups frequently start their sessions by maintaining silence until someone feels a need to say something. This technique (it *is* a technique) has proved to be effective, and it suits the leadership style of certain individuals. We do not challenge the use of silence as a viable technique. If, however, sitting back and waiting is the *only* technique a leader has, we question his or her competency.

The value and purpose of some catalysts may be misinterpreted because they are light, active, fun, and sometimes mistaken for "parlor games." The reader should understand our serious intent in suggesting the use of catalysts. The level of intensity of group interaction can be stimulated and regulated through skillful application of catalysts. The leader is responsible for determining the group's (not the individual's) level of emotional intensity. *Skilled* applications always require the leader to have a clear purpose in mind, an abiding respect for the member's right to refuse to participate, and a sense of timing to determine when the structured activity should yield to natural interpersonal contact.

The importance of employing catalysts sparingly and with clear objectives in mind cannot be stressed too much. Catalysts are a *means* to an end, not an end in themselves. Their purpose is to stimulate meaningful participant interaction. As disclosure increases and interaction becomes more natural and less structured, dedication to the employed catalyst can diminish (Blaker & Samo, 1973).

A leader's insistence on using or completing an exercise may actually detract from spontaneous interaction. In fact, an exercise should be completed only if the group insists on it. For example, imagine that some type of "go-around" catalyst has been introduced and the group's interest has drifted to other issues and concerns stimulated by the activity. Possibly, not all group members will get a chance to have a turn before the session ends. The leader should let the group members express their concerns about not finishing the activity. If the leader senses that someone is feeling left out because he or she did not get a turn, the leader can express this observation and check out what is going on with that particular member. The exercise, however, is *always* secondary to the interaction it stimulates. Futhermore, catalysts are not inherently valuable in themselves; they do not assure meaningful interaction. A skillful leader is required to accomplish that.

One high school counselor's interest in group work was aroused by attending a workshop conducted by one of the authors. She asked for specific advice as to how the exercises should be applied for beginning her group. Six different activities were outlined in a progressive fashion intended to bring her unacquainted group members to a stage of reasonably open interaction. The structured sequence was intended to cover a period of six weeks. Obviously, there was a failure to communicate our progressive model clearly because the counselor called after her first session to request six more exercises. She had used them all. We could only fantasize the frantic pace with which her group members must have engaged themselves in her communication exercises.

CATALYTIC ACTIVITIES

The literature on counseling, human relations training, interpersonal communications skills, encounter groups, and the like offers a cornucopia of techniques and procedures that can be adapted as catalysts for an extensional group. We do not pretend to begin to cover the vast resources available to the reader.[2] We will provide, however, a framework in which to organize the catalysts the reader already possesses and is yet to discover. In order to approach the use of catalytic activities intelligently, so that objectives for using them make sense, it is necessary to have some means of organizing the flood of possibilities available.

In addition to the framework, we will present a sampling of some of the catalytic activities we have found useful. We do not offer them because they are the "best." In fact, we are convinced that leaders who look for techniques and procedures to assure interactive success in group are approaching their work naively.

---

[2] As an example of the abundance of techniques and exercises, we refer to a single source among many. Since 1972, University Associates of San Diego, California, has been publishing voluminous annuals and handbooks entirely devoted to exercises, activities, and materials that are adaptable catalysts (Pfeiffer & Jones, 1972-80).

Techniques and exercises are only as good as the leader applying them. The leader's skill lies in his or her ability to adapt and adjust according to the demands of the moment.

We have adapted a model presented by Trotzer (1977) for categorizing communication exercises, offering examples of each from this chapter. Verbal and nonverbal distinctions are aligned in relation to *inter*personal and *intra*personal focuses. Adding the variable of leader control rounds out Figure 8.1.

FIGURE 8.1
Categorizing Catalytic Activities for Extensional Groups

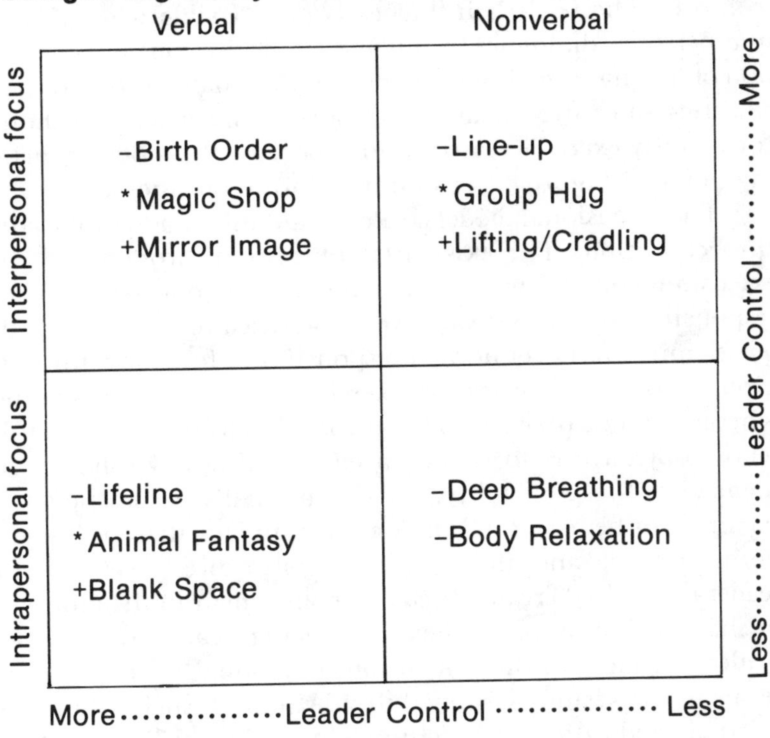

	Verbal	Nonverbal	
Interpersonal focus	-Birth Order *Magic Shop +Mirror Image	-Line-up *Group Hug +Lifting/Cradling	More········Leader Control
Intrapersonal focus	-Lifeline *Animal Fantasy +Blank Space	-Deep Breathing -Body Relaxation	Less········

More ··············Leader Control ············· Less

Adapted from model in Trotzer's (1977) *The Counselor and the Group*, p. 106.

-Low intensity *Medium intensity +High intensity

Leader Control

A brief explanation about leader control is in order before proceeding to an examination of catalysts. In the extensional model the leader is *always in control* of the group process. By "leader control" we are referring to the degree of overt action observed. The more-to-less continua in Figure 8.1 represent the relative amounts of intervention and facilitation the leader engages in. The more *intra*personal and nonverbal the catalyst's effects are, the less "material" there is for a leader to work with (control). The leader's influence is most visible when there is *inter*personal dialogue. In this model, leader control is a function of having something to control rather than meeting responsibilities for control. The "more" does not mean a leader should consciously exert increased control because the model is dictating "more." Figure 8.1 is simply pointing out the obvious.

The extensional model creates an almost paradoxical leadership condition. The existential philosophy from which the extensional model was derived insists that one is ultimately responsible for self; yet we have emphasized repeatedly that the leader must never relinquish responsibility for controlling the group process. *How* leaders exercise control is the issue, not whether or not they should control. The leader, for example, whose objective is to create an encouraging environment for member self-responsibility, may intentionally become less visible in his or her control. It may appear, in fact, that the leader is doing nothing and allowing members to direct events. If the leader has indeed created such an environment in the group, he or she is still in control. When introducing a catalyst, competent leaders are clear in their intentions to gradually withdraw and let members assume responsibility. Although such action may resemble abdication, it is definitely not relinquishing control.

Trotzer's Model

In each cell of the model presented in Figure 8.1, we have included samples of catalytic activities that, along with others, will be described later. The catalysts are organized into four categories:

Interpersonal/Verbal Activities:

Individuals interacting with each other in dialogue — e.g., introducing oneself to the group and answering questions.

Interpersonal/Nonverbal Activities:

Individuals interacting with each other without words — e.g., silent handshakes.

Intrapersonal/Verbal Activities:

Individuals engaging in an exercise that is done alone at first, knowing that the format calls for sharing and exploring with others are a later time — e.g., drawing a "lifeline" to be shared. The drawing is completed alone. The explanation of it is verbal.

Intrapersonal/Nonverbal Activities:

Individuals engaging in an activity that, by design, is intended to be a private, personal experience — e.g., prayer. (Extensional groups in church settings frequently use prayer as a catalytic activity.)

Although each of the cells in Figure 8.1 contains catalysts that can be of immense personal value, the group is concerned primarily with interactive components of the model. Even if the group engages in nonverbal exercises, the very nature of group work implies sharing and offering each other feedback during and after the activity. Spontaneous use of catalytic activities is preferred over preplanned, highly structured catalysts. Therefore, the catalysts in the following pages intentionally exclude activities that require equipment (e.g., masks, slides, boffers, paints, butcher paper). Paper, pencil, and pieces of construction paper are the only exceptions.

The catalytic activities vary in their potential for stimulating interaction. Some catalysts (e.g., "Birth Order") are patently low-keyed. Others, such as "Lifting" and "Cradling," are designed to evoke interaction of great intensity. Although quantifying an activity's potential is difficult, we have attempted to *generally* estimate each activity's potential in terms of low-medium-high intensity. A simple catalyst may, for some reason, become surprisingly powerful in generating feelings with a person or among the group. And "heavy" catalysts fall like a dud on occasion, although they may have worked dependably in the past.

Several of the catalytic activities call for group members to express thoughts, opinions, and insights about other group members. It is *absolutely essential* that the leader concentrate on the idea that the speaker is speaking about himself or herself. The recipient of the thoughts, opinions, and insights may react in a positive or negative manner. When and if the recipient responds, the recipient is speaking about himself or herself.

We tend to discourage the use of high-intensity (+) catalysts early in a group. A reasonable amount of interaction is required before the bonds of trust begin to develop among members. The leader's skill, sensitivity, and courage are the major influences in determining success when using catalysts. The reader can appreciate the impossibility of accurately predicting on an *a priori* basis how effective a catalyst will be. The site, group purpose, and relative maturity of the group's participations are crucial considerations for determining the "right" catalyst for the "right" moment.

INTERPERSONAL/VERBAL ACTIVITIES

(−) Low Intensity

(−) Birth Order

A simple but usually productive device to encourage group members to look at themselves is to ask the group to subdivide into small groups according to whether the member was first born, last born, or middle born. Members of each group discuss problems that occurred in their lives as a result of their sibling position. Then the entire group reassembles to share points of view. This technique focuses attention on present perceptions of group members as they talk about a productive topic of group content — individual members.

(-) Territoriality

Asking a group that has been in session at least twice to change seats after the group has started will bring up the import of territoriality. Did group members tend to arrange themselves in the same seating order each time? How did they feel when they saw someone else sitting in their "territory?" Who sat next to whom after the rearrangement? What is each member's psychological territory? Acceptable social distances might be discussed before focusing on how close to some group members other specific group members can sit without becoming uncomfortable. The discussion of variations in distance can lead to confrontations between group members. Another illustration of territoriality results from asking group members to whisper in each other's ear and then to talk nose-to-nose.

(-) First Memories

Members share with the group their first memories of conflict. What was significant about those memories? Do group members perceive similarities in current behavior patterns that might create conflict?

(-) Free Association

Free association can stimulate confrontation. The usual procedure is for the group leader to present a stimulus word that may or may not be "loaded" and ask group members to respond quickly around the circle. (The leader should note split-second censoring and perhaps call it to the group's attention.) This technique tends to bring out affective content and is useful as a warmup process. "Going-around" is seldom completed more

169

than a time or two before the group is dealing with significant materials.

(-) Druthers . . .

The go-around begins the sentence stem: "If I had my druthers, I would be right now . . ." This fantasy may help members explore their value systems, action choices, and self-acceptance.

(-) Symbolic Substitution

Asking each member to fantasize what animal, or bird, or building, or geometric figure, or plant, or color, he or she would like to be is often productive as members crystallize their perceptions of who they are. In using this game, each member must direct the symbolic substitution to self; members should not be permitted to label other members as an animal, or whatever.

(-) New Names

Another helpful way of exploring the sense of self is to have members each select a new name for themselves, to be used in that group session. The group is asked to react to those names. Again, members should select their own names; others should not choose for them.

(-) Best Possible Way of Life

Asking members to describe their best possible way of life and then, perhaps, their worst possible way of life, may help them identify where they are now on this continuum.

170

(-) Yes-No

This invigorating exercise is fun, and it can bring insight into suppressed aggressive feelings. In pairs, one group member is "yes" and the other is "no." One starts by whispering "yes," and the partner responds with "no." The responses are to intensify, ending with loud shouts after five or six exchanges. When the excitement dies down after the last exchange, the partners reverse roles and go through the procedure again.

(-) Pair and Share

In an excellent get-acquainted activity if participants in first sessions are strangers, the leader instructs members to each find one other person they would like to get to know. The pairs have approximately ten minutes in which to get acquainted. They are then instructed to find another pair they think might be interesting. The leader should allow sufficient time for members to introduce their partners to the other pairs.

(-) Labeling

An enjoyable way for group members to learn each other's names in an opening group session is to have them select an adjective or descriptive label that precedes their name — e.g., "I'm Studious Stan," "I'm Beer-Drinking Phil," "I'm Nervous Betty." A variation of this exercise is to "go-around" the group, with members stating as many previously offered labels and names as they can before revealing their own.

(-) Three Adjectives

In a "go-around" procedure, each member is asked to describe himself or herself using three adjectives. The group interacts as each member offers these descriptive adjectives.

171

(-) Appreciate-Regret

This exercise can be used constructively at various stages of the group's development, from beginning to closing. It is a semi-structured activity that gives members permission to express themselves in the here and now. When a session has been centered for a long time on one individual, or the group has dwelt a long time on one theme or topic, the "appreciate-regret" activity allows all members to contribute something, however brief.

The task is simple. Members are free to make as many statements as they wish that begin with, "I appreciate . . ." and/or "I regret . . . " This may be confused with *capping* (Chapter 4). The difference lies in the activity's time perspective. Capping is designed to bring members' focus away from the here and now by reviewing thoughts and impressions that have taken place in the group, in preparation for closing. In contrast, this activity focuses on *present* thoughts and feelings as they occur.

(-) Elephant-Giraffe

A silly, laugh-provoking, energizing activity may be useful for a tepid group, such as sometimes is the case after lunch. This is also an entertaining way to create a new mix of members when the leader senses that cliques may be forming when members habitually sit in the same place. After the activity, the leader instructs members to be seated right where they are.

Initially, a standing circle is formed with the leader in the center. He or she appoints a member in the circle to be a "demonstrator-elephant." An elephant can be symbolized by putting fist-on-fist against the nose to represent a trunk. Members on each side of the designated "elephant" to help out by placing their hands by the "elephant's" ears as if to magnify the impression of big ears. A "demonstrator-giraffe" is then selected and instructed to stretch his or her clasped hands high over the head to signify the giraffe's long neck. The "giraffe's" adjacent

172

members help out by touching the "giraffe's" knees to denote the giraffe's long legs.

The leader continues to randomly assign group members as "elephant" or "giraffe." The designees and their two "neighbors" must act instantly to do what is necessary to become an "elephant" or a "giraffe." If either the designee or neighbor fails to respond quickly and correctly, the leader can decide to exchange places with that member.

The fun part is surprising a person in the circle with a quick, sharp command that allows little time to think. For example, the person in the center may bark the command, "ELEPHANT!" to a member in the circle, who immediately shoots both hands toward the ceiling (error), while one neighbor touches his ear (correct) and the other touches her knee (error). The person in the center arbitrarily decides which of the two errors deserves placement in the center. If the group is large (fifteen or more), the leader can place two (or more) members in the center of the circle.

This is a fast-moving, physically stimulating activity, and even the most reserved group member usually enjoys the laughter and stimulation. The leader should not carry the activity on too long, however, because it does tend to lose its zest after a while.

(–) True-False

This "go-around" activity permits self-disclosure and feedback in an indirect way. Someone (usually the leader) starts by describing something about himself or herself that may be either true or fabricated — e.g., "I have appeared in movies" (followed with details). When finished, other group members react with their judgments as to whether the person has told the truth or not. The important part of this exercise is the responders' reasoning as to why they think the person's statement is true or false.

173

(-) Color Cards

Small strips, bits, pieces, and sections of multicolored construction paper are placed in the center of the group. The leader instructs participants to "close your eyes, reflect back over the day's experiences, and try to get in touch with your feelings of this moment. As you do this, try to picture [this is a good exercise for visually oriented people] color(s) that represent your feelings. Also try to picture if your feelings are big or small, jagged or smooth, linear or round, and so forth. When you open your eyes, select color(s) and shape(s) that best match your awareness." The leader then asks group members to explain or describe the pieces of construction paper they have selected.

(-) Presentation of Self: Clothing

The leader begins by suggesting that members make a statement about themselves in the clothing they are wearing. In introductory remarks, the leader might say, "From an almost infinite variety of possibilities, we selected (or someone else selected — which is significant) a wardrobe. Then, from the variety in our wardrobe, we selected the clothes we are wearing right now. Each of us is making some statements about self through our clothing and it might be productive to suggest what *you* see yourself transmitting by your clothes today."

The leader should begin by suggesting ideas about his or her own clothes. For example, a male leader might see himself as "conservative," because of his vest and gray suit, but a little rebellious because of his choice of tie. As members explore their presentations of self, the leader should generalize to a characteristic way of behaving, then to a life-style.

Medium Intensity (*)

(*) Taking a Trip

Ask the group members to imagine that they are going to take a trip to a place of their choosing and that they can take two people along from the group. Whom would each member select? What is the reaction of those selected?

(*) Strength Bombardment

Members individually volunteer to tell what their own personal strengths are, and the group responds by telling what strengths they see in these volunteers. The leader may want to be the first volunteer. The member or leader may extend the exchange by asking, "What do you see as preventing me/you from using those strengths?"

(*) Self-Report

This exercise involves a "go-around." Each group member is asked to make a specified number of statements about self, which should be personal: "I am a damned good teacher," "I should be a better parent," "I am feeling overwhelmed by all my responsibilities." The group then reacts. The leader should set the stage by being the first to make the self-report.

A variation of this procedure involves use of a timer, such as a small hourglass sand timer. Each member talks about himself or herself during the time allotted.

(*) Metaphors

A catalyst that can be used in the total group or in subgroups (subgroups are a common procedure for early sessions), this activity involves participants forming impressions in their minds of their group mates and trying to associate food, animal, automobile, weather, color, or any item that metaphorically summarizes their impressions. In sharing the metaphor, the most important part is to give the reasoning for the metaphor (e.g., "You seem like a teddy bear; you're physically powerful looking but very gentle in disposition").

175

(*) Significant Moment

Members are asked to reflect back in memory to a time, person, or event(s) that proved to have a significant influence on the member's present situation. In accordance with the here-and-now emphasis of extensional groups, the leader tries to help the group use past experiences to stimulate discussion about the member's *present*.

(*) As a Group Member

Toward the end of the group experience, a good activity is to ask members to complete the sentence, "As a group member, I . . ." This triggers exploration of the meaning of the group for each participant, the commitment he or she has to the group, and perhaps what the member wants or has obtained from the sessions.

(*) Freezing

When group content seems to be drifting off to the there and then, the leader might ask members to "freeze" and to elicit feedback from members about their feelings.

(*) Magic Shop

The approach in this activity is to ask members to imagine they can shop at a magic place that stocks only intangibles. Any intangible, such as honesty, love, or great intelligence, may be purchased, but the price is something intangible that the individual already owns — such as good health or joy of living. This is an excellent device to confront group members with their value systems and the commitment each may have to any given set of values.

A possible variation is to suggest that members may obtain anything from the Magic Shop but need not return anything. Or they may exchange something they wish to discard for something in the "shop."

(*) Role-playing

A effective group technique, but one too infrequently used in group counseling, is role-playing. An alert leader can easily find appropriate situations for role-playing, arising out of content that group members provide. The technique of role reversal is important, as is sufficient time in the group session to thoroughly explore the implications of the role play. Insights gained through skillful use of this technique usually are highly satisfactory.

High Intensity (+)

(+) I Have a Secret

This exercise provides an opportunity for deeper, more intimate self-disclosure than is the goal in the previously discussed activities. One outcome is that participants usually discover that their "secrets" are not so unusual. Each member briefly describes a "secret" on a piece of paper. All the papers are placed in a pile. No names are used so that the secrets can be discussed freely. If a member chooses to reveal his or her identity, or if a member chooses not to participate but does not want the rest of the group to know, these personal choices must be honored. A volunteer selects a "secret" from the stack, reads it, and offers his or her commentary. The group is then free to talk about the "secret" or whatever topic it stimulates among the group. A variation of this is "Fears Anonymous," using the same approach but with a more specific focus.

(+) Farewell

An excellent catalyst for a closing session, this activity permits members to express feelings they have not yet shared. The instructions are: "This is our last session together. Some of us may not see each other again. Take a few minutes to reflect on what messages you would like to leave."

Members who have had a meaningful group experience sometimes become quite emotional in doing this exercise. The leader should participate, too, but not to the extent that he or she is unavailable to members who are emotional, or to members who may need encouragement to share their farewell messages.

A variation of this exercise is to have everyone stand in a circle and express farewells nonverbally as well as verbally. This can be an equally, if not more, emotional experience.

(+) *Most/Least Like Me*

A catalyst that requires some degree of courage by participants calls for identifying group mates who have characteristics that the speaker thinks represent or do not represent his or her own. Examples are: "Sam seems to have the same difficulty as I have about being open in this group." "Sharon's deep religious beliefs do not match with my avoidance of formalized religion."

(+) *Choosing a Family*

Members select a "family" from group members — a mother, father, younger sibling, older sibling, spouse, son, and daughter. For the purposes of this exercise, the sex of group members is ignored. The group then discusses the selections. The degree of frankness with which the procedure is carried out depends on the group leader.

(+) *Personal Constructs*

Three students who are interested in learning the impression the group has of them volunteer to be "targets." The group then suggests ways in which any two of the three volunteers are alike or different from the third. This exercise focuses on the here and now of the group process and group members — the level at which behavioral change is most likely to take place.

(+) Mirror Image

Group members are asked individually to look at themselves in a mirror (a hand mirror is simple and effective) and describe what they see as honestly as they can. Members then give feedback, agreeing or disagreeing, with reasons given.

(+) First Impressions

Members are asked to recall and report uncensored their first impressions of others in the group. This must be done on a highly personal level to be productive.

(+) Legitimizing

A useful "go-around" is to ask each member to specify a personal characteristic that he or she feels a need to legitimize. For example, Rick might suggest that he feels his need to manipulate and his need to exert his sexuality may need legitimizing; that is, he feels they are a part of him that is not accepted by others. Group members can give their reactions to the member's quest. Leaders should be alert at this point so that members do not begin "super-mothering" in an effort to legitimize. Super-mothering involves a denial of a member's reality; legitimizing involves complete acceptance and recognition of that member's reality.

INTERPERSONAL/NONVERBAL ACTIVITIES

Low Intensity (-)

(-) Danish Thumb Wrestle

This activity is useful when leaders think hidden aggressions and hostilities might be successfully explored nonverbally.

179

The exercise may involve the entire group or only two members. Those involved form dyads, interlace their fingers, and touch thumbs, using one hand only. Each member of the pair then attempts to force the other's thumb down for a count of three by applying pressure on the thumb. The discussion that follows the exercise should uncover hidden feelings of animosity between members.

A variation of this activity does not necessarily focus on hostility or aggression but on various kinds of nonverbal interpersonal contact. With fingers interlaced, thumbs *touching* (not suppressing), the participants close their eyes and, through the thumbs, send messages the leader suggests: "Hello," "Get out of my way, please," "I like you very much," and so on.

(-) *Line-up*

This exercise can be adapted to any theme in which members are looking for nonverbal ways of comparing themselves with group mates. In the initial instruction the members are told that they must stand in a straight line, shoulder to shoulder. They can change their relative positions in the line, but this may cause other members to have to move from their positions. No doubling up in the same spot is permitted. There can be only one person per place. The line may represent a continuum of control — e.g., "The people who are at this end of the line are the most controlling group members here, and the one at the very end is admitting that he [or she] wishes to control *every*one else in the line." The themes can be love, fearfulness, sexiness — anything that seems relevant to the group's concern of the moment.

(-) *Hand Mirroring*

As an energizing, enjoyable, nonverbal activity, this one is excellent. It also may produce some interesting dominance-submission insights.

180

Partners stand facing each other with ample room for moving about. They are instructed to put their hands up, palms out, matching each other's palms but not touching. They are to imagine that powerful rubber bands connect their wrists, pulling their palms toward their partner's. *But,* if their palms make contact, they will have completed an electrical circuit that gives them both a painful shock. They can avoid the shock by keeping their palms from touching, but the "rubber bands" keep pulling their palms together.

After preliminary instructions, the participants are told to explore their space together — up, down, around. They are also free to move about the room, provided that they remain in the palm-facing-palm position. Some hilarious impromptu dances sometimes result.

(-) Changing Seats

One exercise that can be useful in understanding territoriality behavior is for leaders to ask members of a group that has been in session for a time (perhaps a half-hour) to change seats. This can be done by asking the entire group to change places at one time, or perhaps by going around the circle and asking each member in turn to select the place of another member (or leader) as his or her territory.

After either approach, members discuss the experience and the meaning it had for them. The continuums of dominance-submission, independence-dependence, competition-cooperation, the issues of aggression, timidity, authority figure perceptions, sex roles, and extent of each member's life-space are only a few of the possibilities for discussion. *A word of caution:* The leader should not feel it is necessary to introduce the foregoing topics; rather, members should verbalize their reactions to the experience, and the leader should help them see the meanings of their behaviors at whatever level seems appropriate to the maturity and psychological sophistication of the group.

Medium Intensity (*)

(*) Mill-in

An exercise that touches the concept of territoriality has members drift about the room for an unspecified time. The leader deliberately avoids presenting any limits. Eventually each member will establish a "territory," either as part of a subgroup or individually, standing or sitting. How long did it take? How did members feel about the lack of a set agenda? How did they structure their physical fields? How do they handle this situation in life outside the group? How do they handle time outside the group? How close did people stand together? Was this culturally determined?

(*) Group Hug

This is a nice way to end a session that has been especially warm and caring. The group is asked to stand, joining in a circle with arms about members on either side of them to tighten the circle. Often, as the group becomes physically tighter, a natural rocking motion begins. The rocking is sometimes accompanied by a humming sound that emerges naturally.

(*) Blind Walk

This is a standard human relations training exercise that is a dependable discussion starter. For half of the group, blindfolding or simply closing the eyes makes the "blinded" person dependent upon his or her guide partner. Five to ten minutes are allotted for exploring. Outside of the building is interesting to explore if trees, walks, benches, or other such features are present. Exploring hallways, water fountains, and stairs is good also. After the initial time period has elapsed, the "blind" person should switch roles and become the guide. Discussions about honesty, dependence, independence, and responsibility are common results of this experience.

(*) Circle Massage

Group members stand in a circle shoulder to shoulder. Then they turn right-face and begin thumping gently on the back of the person in front of them in a rapid staccato manner, moving all around the person's back. Then they switch to neck and shoulder massages for about thirty seconds. The circle often begins to move around of its own volition. After a suitable time period, the leader directs the group to turn about-face and repeat the same process.

(*) Two-foot Square

A square that is much too small to easily accommodate the number of people in the group (a two-foot square for ten people) is marked off. The group's task is to get everyone in the group inside the square. If the group is outdoors, a large stone or stump can be used for the same purpose. An interesting outgrowth of this activity is that it often points out the need for cooperation and cohesiveness to facilitate effective group interaction.

(*) Eye Contact

This is a good exercise for testing sensitivity to nonverbal facial messages. Members come into contact with their feelings about being looked at by another and looking at another. Group members form pairs and silently look into each other's eyes for thirty seconds. Over several group meetings, leaders may want to gradually lengthen the time interval to increasing levels at which members are comfortable with the process and communicating with eye contact becomes routine group behavior. This exercise usually encourages members to become more open with, and sensitive to, others.

183

(*) Trust

The experience of trust can be explored through a nonverbal exercise that asks a member to fall backward into the arms of another without hesitation. Receiving members break the fall with their arms. Many members are unable to fall back without first checking to see if the other person is there. Others cannot allow themselves to fall at all. (Very small people should not attempt to catch very large people but, in general, most people can catch one another without danger to either.) The subsequent discussion gives insight into the ability to trust and general views of the trustworthiness of others. The life-styles of members in relation to their perceptions of others will probably emerge.

(*) Break-in

"Break-in" is a standard nonverbal exercise used to illustrate and explore feelings of rejection and isolation. Members are asked to stand in a tight circle, and one person is left outside the circle. That person attempts to penetrate the group in any way he or she can. This exercise can become quite active, so appropriate precautions should be taken to ensure safety.

Although all members are aware that the experience is contrived, the person who experiences the isolation and rejection may be left with strong feelings, so leaders must be careful to provide ample opportunity for discussion. This activity can be used as a springboard for members to explore their feelings of being rejected, or "outgroup," by the current group, or in their lives outside the group. The concept of territoriality to define ingroup-outgroup lines can be explored.

High Intensity (+)

(+) Lifting

If circumstances are appropriate, the lifting exercise can be used by leaders who want to explore trust in the group as a whole or in certain members. This activity also tends to increase members' feelings of belonging to the group. Members stand in a circle shoulder to shoulder and facing inward; one member stands in the center inside the circle, with eyes closed. When the member in the middle feels relaxed, the members of the circle pass the person in the center one to another for a brief time and then gently lift him or her up over their heads, moving the person back and forth in a swaying motion. The exercise concludes with the group lowering the member to the floor slowly and gently.

The entire exercise is done in complete silence. Verbalizing begins only when all those who wish to have been in the center of the circle. The discussion may center on an individual member's difficulty in trusting.

(+) Cradling and Rocking

This exercise is usually connected with the *lifting* exercise above. As the lifted person is lowered, the group begins a rocking motion. Sometimes after the lifted person has been rocked and lowered to the floor, the exercise ends with the group lightly massaging and stroking the person. All this is done in silence. The person receiving the attention usually prefers to experience it with closed eyes. If the lifted-cradled-rocked-stroked person does not feel that he or she belongs after *this* experience, it is unusual, indeed!

(+) Territoriality

The group is divided in half. One half lines up facing the other across the room. Members extend their arms in front of them and start moving slowly toward the opposite side of the room (a la Frankenstein). They are instructed to take a straight path, and it should lead them to confront someone opposite from them. They will have to decide how to handle the encounter, because they are not permitted to lower their arms or to deviate from a straight path.

The resulting discussion usually starts with identifying "cheaters" (people who allow their paths to vary to avoid physically confronting someone from across the room) and invariably gets around to talking about the embarrassment of confronting someone with outstretched arms. Hugging is one natural outcome; others stop, touching hands, unwilling to enter more closely into another's space.

(+) Nonverbal Encounter

In this exercise a member who has something to express toward another group member is asked to volunteer. The volunteer and the partner stand at opposite ends of the room and slowly approach each other before the entire group. The ensuing encounter is completely nonverbal. When the pair has finished, each discusses his or her feelings, and the whole group discusses its observations. In this way, the participants become aware of messages that might otherwise escape their notice.

(+) Nonverbal Go-around

The opportunity for each group member and the leader to communicate nonverbally with all other group members sets the stage for an intense experience. The group leader asks all members to stand up and move into a comfortable, close circle, facing inward, shoulders almost touching. Each member in turn steps into the inner perimeter of the circle and, facing outward, moves from one member to another, attempting to communicate nonverbally his or her feelings for each member. The leader begins this exercise and, thus, sets the tone. The entire exercise is completed in silence. When everyone has had an opportunity to interact with each other, members take their seats and discuss the experience. Most groups find this a deeply moving experience, and the subsequent discussion usually demonstrates increased group solidarity and heightened sensitivity to each other.

(+) Feeling Space

Another exercise in the area of territoriality involves asking group members to close their eyes and explore the space about them while remaining seated or standing and silent. They should be directed to feel down, back, up, to the side. About three minutes should be allotted for this. Leaders should keep their eyes open so that they can observe, making suggestions when necessary. Members commonly "peek," trying to assess what others are doing and how much "safe" space is available. After the activity is over, the leader(s) can gently encourage members to talk about their discomfort at not knowing what is transpiring while their eyes are closed. The *discussion* is far more important than the fact that a member "cheated."

The discussion should center on members' reactions, especially those experienced when contact was made with another person, or was not made. How did members feel when they found someone else within their territory? How did they feel about temporary isolation from visual contact? How do they handle isolation elsewhere? What are their solitude needs? What are their companionship needs? How did they feel about making contact with a female? A male? The possibilities for discussion are infinite. Leaders must draw upon their art of group leadership for direction.

(+) Finger Point

This exercise helps focus awareness of here-and-now feelings. It also stimulates discussion of attitudes toward fellow group members. Group members are instructed to pull the circle in tightly and then to look about to see where each member is in the group. The instructions are:

"Close your eyes. Picture the group as we are sitting here in our circle. Think about your group mates. We've been together now for - - - -. What are some of your impressions and feelings toward other

187

group members? Are there some for whom you have particularly warm feelings? Where, in your mind, are these people sitting right now?

"There are probably several people here for whom you have good feelings, but try to concentrate on just one of those persons. Where, in your mind, is that person seated right now? Try to picture it. Without opening your eyes, point to where you think that person is seated. Don't open your eyes, just point . . . hold your point without opening your eyes . . . (Very abruptly) OK, open your eyes! Hold your finger where it is for a moment."

This game obviously may provoke rather intense feelings. The leader should monitor the body language occurring during the exercise, such as heavy breathing and crossing of arms and legs, to obtain some indication of how much stress or tension individual group members are experiencing. Sometimes members cannot keep their eyes closed because of the anxiety. Under no circumstances should pressure be applied to make members conform.

Another version of the finger point activity is to substitute negative feelings for positive feelings. This also requires good leadership skills and careful monitoring.

INTRAPERSONAL/VERBAL ACTIVITIES

Low Intensity (–)

(–) Lifeline

Although it is an effective exercise for helping members get better acquainted, this is not appropriate as an introductory activity. Members are to draw a line on a piece of paper, left to right, that reflects the ups and downs of their lives. Afterward, members explain their lines to the others. Listeners are encouraged to ask questions, and presenters are encouraged to elaborate on their lines. It is desirable, sometimes, to break the larger group into subgroups of three to five participants. In this exercise smaller groupings tend to maintain stimulation of interaction, while large groups permit too much anonymity.

A variation is to review one's life as a series of critical incidents that stand out in one's memory. On a blank piece of paper each member places a dot on the left-hand side to represent birth. Without lifting the pen or pencil, members depict in graphlike fashion the progress of their lives — the highs, low, and various "in-betweens." Critical incidents in a member's life usually are represented by peaks or valleys in the uninterrupted line. This "road of life" serves as a source for discussion as members share commonalities and differences in their "roads."

(-) Perfect Day

This activity encourages members to share their values and interests in life outside the group. It is also an excellent catalyst for helping members recognize and accept members whose values are different from their own.

The instructions are: "All of us have preferences as to how we like to spend our time. But we often have responsibilities that prevent us from doing what we would really like to be doing. If you had the freedom, time, and money to plan a day that is perfect for you, what would it look like?" After they have been allowed quiet time to think, members are given paper and pencil and asked to jot down their thoughts about a perfect day. These thoughts are shared later with the group.

Medium Intensity (*)

(*) Childhood Rediscovery Fantasy

Group members relax and mentally prepare themselves for fantasizing. The leader says, "In your fantasy, recall a particular moment of joy . . . of sorrow in your childhood. What would you have changed if you had such power?

Other childhood rediscovery fantasies might have themes of:

> cleaning out the attic, basement, garage, closet, etc. (What do you discover/rediscover?)
>
> being in a costume room, free to dress in any manner you choose.
>
> animals in your childhood that you enjoyed/avoided. (What was it about them that affected you the way they did?)

(*) Animal Fantasy

Although this exercise can be done quickly, it seems to have the most impact when participants can spend some quiet time thinking about animals they would like to be if reincarnated. In their reflective time, they are to think of the qualities of the animal they admire/respect/detest most.

(*) Autobiographies

The capsule autobiography can be used to effect confrontation. Each group member is asked to write five or six sentences concerning his or her life history. The leader reads these aloud, without identifying the writers. Discussion follows each reading. Is there a life theme (a script)? Group members can gain understanding of the life-space of other group members and may also obtain insight into their own life-space. A focus may also be on future plans. Confrontation will be elicited through this exercise if the group leader is familiar with projective theory.

(*) Symbolic Objects

The leader begins the group by asking each member to select some concrete thing or things from the environment that symbolize himself or herself. The area from which to select can be as extensive as time and area allow.

When members return to the group, they each present their object and describe how that object symbolizes themselves. The leader should make a selection, too, and begin the interaction by his or her presentation. For example, the leader might have chosen a set of keys. Then he or she might describe these keys as representing a personal search for answers, always looking for ways to open doors to truth, or looking for ways to unlock relationships with people, or feeling a need for protection or isolation.

(*) What Would You Like to Be Remembered For?

In this activity, members explore the memories of themselves that they would like to stand on as their "signatures of essence." This helps participants identify their value structures and the ways in which they are translating those values into action. For instance, one member might want to be remembered for the friends he made, another for the fact that she loved someone very deeply. Some members might not want to be remembered at all. Whatever statements are made can be explored productively.

High Intensity (+)

(+) Gestalt Chairs

This technique is commonly used in gestalt therapeutic approaches. It is normal for an individual to be in conflict between two incompatible situations or conditions. A choice must be made and acted upon, but confusion at having two desirable (or sometimes undesirable) choices seems insurmountable. The person in conflict is asked to sit in one of two chairs and speak from one of the points of view. Then he or she switches to the other chair and speaks from the opposing point of view. When the individual feels that the issue has been thoroughly "debated," he or she elicits feedback from the group.

This is a powerfully effective technique, regardless of the nature of the conflict. It could be as simple as a young man trying to decide about asking a particular girl for a date, or as complex and intense as a young woman deciding whether or not to become a nun.

(+) *Twenty-four Hours to Live*

The leader fantasizes that the group has discovered that each member has only the next twenty-four hours to live. The participants in turn describe how they would spend the time.

(+) *New Ways of Behaving*

For a specified time, group members try out a way of behaving that they consider desirable, but which they have not previously tried. Five minutes may be sufficient for the exercise if the group is not too large. At the end of the designated time, members are asked to report to the group what "new" behaviors they observed in others, to react to their own "new" behavior, and to report the feelings involved. Some members might not be able to identify "new" ways to behave. This realization constitutes an important area for discussion.

(+) *Blank Space*

Each member has a blank sheet of paper on which to project his or her life-space. Several minutes of silence are allowed to do this. Then the leader asks members to describe whatever elements on their paper they wish to. As members complete their descriptions, the leader asks for feedback to that member before moving on to another person. Leaders facilitate the understanding of life-styles, values, and so forth by their verbal reactions, performing both the modeling and facilitating functions.

A refinement of this procedure is to ask that each member do something physically with the sheet of paper at the end of his or her presentation. A member might throw it on the floor, sit on it, hold it close to the body, or hold it out to others. Whatever he or she does provides profound material for exploration and legitimizing.

INTRAPERSONAL/NONVERBAL ACTIVITIES

Low Intensity (-)

(-) Deep Breathing

Deep breathing exercises can be used to open a group session once a group has been taught the technique. It is quite different from the usual process of respiration, which moves air vigorously in and out of the nostrils. The "yoga" approach to deep breathing involves a "tuning in" to one's inner world of proprioception and, in particular, to the expansion and contraction feelings of the rib-cage that accompany breathing. Members are directed to fill the lower part of their lungs with air first, then the middle part, and finally the upper part. In exhaling, the upper part, then the middle, and then the lower part of the lungs is emptied. The chest remains motionless and passive while the ribs expand during inhalation and contract during exhalation. Members breathe in to the count of four, hold for two counts, and exhale to four counts. Ten or twelve deep breaths are relaxing and help members get in touch with the rib-cage and lungs. A more extensive description of the techniques of deep breathing can be found in Devi's book, *Yoga for Americans* (1959).

(-) Body Relaxation

An exercise that can follow the few minutes of deep breathing involves the leader asking members to sit up straight in their chairs and put both feet flat on the floor, with closed eyes. (In an appropriate setting, this exercise can be done with members lying flat on their backs on the floor.) The leader then "talks" quietly up the body, beginning with the feet, asking members to relax the muscles in their left foot, then the right foot. Next the leader moves to the left and right lower legs, knees, and so on. This is done slowly, and members' eyes remain closed throughout the entire exercise. The period ends with a few minutes of silence. This procedure allows members to get in touch with their bodies, as well as to relax their muscle systems.

SUMMARY

The preceding catalysts may be useful in encouraging a group to focus on the here and now, I and Thou, but the main instrument of movement toward confrontation is the group leader. If the leader is willing to risk self in encounter, the group is likely to follow. If the leader is not, the group probably will remain at a safe, nonproductive, topic-centered level.

REFERENCES

Blaker, Kenneth E., and Samo, Jan. "Communications Games: A Group Counseling Technique," *The School Counselor,* Vol. 21 (1973), pp. 46-51.

Devi, Indra. *Yoga For Americans.* Englewood-Cliffs, NJ: Prentice-Hall, 1959.

Elliott, James. *Personal Growth Through Guided Imagery.* Berkeley, CA: Explorations Institute, 1976.

Lewis, Howard R., and Streitfeld, Harold S. *Growth Games: How To Tune In Yourself, Your Family, Your Friends.* New York: Harcourt, Brace, Jovanovich, 1970.

Pfeiffer, William J., and Jones, John E. *A Handbook of Structured Experiences for Human Relations Training* (Vols. I-VIII). San Diego, CA: University Associates, 1972-80.

_____. *Annual Handbook for Group Facilitators* (Vols. I-VIII). San Diego, CA: University Associates, Inc., 1972-80.

Stevens, John. *Awareness: Exploring, Experimenting, Experiencing.* Moab, UT: Real People Press, 1971.

Trotzer, James P. *The Counselor and The Group.* Belmont, CA: Wadsworth Publishing Co., 1977.

9

The Extensional Group Model in Educational Settings

9

The Extensional Group Model
in Educational Settings

Educational settings can be defined as elementary school (grades K through 6), middle school (7-8/9) and senior high school (9/10-12). Obviously, individual and group characteristics overlap enormously, and the authors have attempted to be sufficiently general to absorb much of the overlap. For that reason, this chapter differentiates between elementary and high school levels only.

What might appear to be a disproportionate amount of attention to the elementary school level is actually a result of its being the first to be described in this chapter. Many of the ideas explained in the elementary school section are adaptable to the high school section. We have attempted to minimize repetition. Also, younger aged groups require considerably more pre-planned structure than do older groups.

The extensional group model applied to young children still depends heavily on self-disclosure and feedback, but younger members are more dependent on structured activities and prepared materials for achieving interaction. This does not mean that younger children cannot interact spontaneously or that older members cannot profit from structured activities. *Generally*, the catalytic activities presented in Chapter 8, because of their spontaneous applications, become more effective as the age of the group increases.

ELEMENTARY SCHOOL GROUP COUNSELING

Group counseling with elementary school-age children is, in essence, no different from counseling in groups with participants of any age. The extensional group model is appropriate for any group leader who is working with members who want to extend their abilities to function in the world, whether the members are students of elementary school age, secondary school age, college age, or not students at all. But some special considerations might be given to groups composed of elementary school-age children.

Special Considerations in Elementary School Counseling Groups

In an elementary school-age counseling group, there are some special concerns that are not likely to occur with older group members. *The importance of preserving the integrity of the home and family is vital, and the leader must make sure that the young student does not discuss concerns that would violate this privacy.* Elementary school children cannot be expected to have the degree of social sophistication that older students have; thus, the leader must vigorously protect their privacy and that of their families. This may involve more frequent intervention than is usually necessary when working with an older group.

Leaders of elementary school counseling groups should observe some important parameters that derived from the developmental age of these young students. Redl (1966) suggested that the way a counseling group of children is put together must not be left to chance. The composition of a group may be of great importance of the kind of group life that will develop and the effects the group will have on its members. Among students of this age bracket, the possibilities of "contagion" are greater than they are when students are older. Therefore, children ought not be put into a group where they do not belong, because they will either seriously disturb the group or will suffer damage through exposure to the wrong group life. Redl believes that students should not be too far removed from one another in terms of toughness, physical prowess, sex sophistication, and developmental stage. If a leader finds that a student has been misplaced in a counseling group, he or she should confer with that student privately and remove the student from the group.

Redl's life-space interview (1959) was directed toward work on an individual basis, but the goals he specified for the single interview are applicable to the goals of group counseling with elementary school children. Through the group process, students can experience a reality "rub-in," in Redl's terms, which will help youngsters who habitually misinterpret interpersonal situations (e.g., those who think the teacher is always "against" them) derive more appropriate meanings from social situations. Through group interaction, students can come to see that a maladaptive style of life really involves more secondary pains than gains. Through group, a child can learn other, more satisfying ways of behaving, and can expand psychological boundaries to include other adults and teachers. Group can also help a child come to accept aspects of self that were formerly unacceptable.

Redl identified elements of emotional first aid that are relevant to the group process in elementary schools. These applications include: draining off hostilities and daily frustrations so they do not accumulate to an intolerable degree; providing emotional support when children are overwhelmed by feelings of panic or guilt; offering a relationship that keeps the child from retreating into his or her own world as a consequence of emotional upheaval; governing social traffic so as to remind children of "house" policies and regulations; and serving as a "forum" in which to work out feelings about disputes, fights, and other "loaded transactions."

Some special considerations must be observed when organizing and conducting groups composed of elementary school children. The size of the group and the length of each session depend on the ages of the children. For example, in early childhood (ages five through nine) the group should contain only three or four members, carefully selected so as not to include more than one aggressive child and not more than one extremely passive child. For primary-age children, group sessions should probably not be longer than twenty to thirty minutes. The process and content of the elementary school group also may differ from those of other groups.

Elementary school groups, particularly those at the youngest levels, require considerably more structure and preplanning of activities than do groups of older children. Puppets (Dinkmeyer, 1973), "Magic Circles" (Bessell & Palomares, 1970), role plays, sociodrama, open-ended stories, and art work are suggested catalysts for young children's groups. Videotape is an excellent tool and one to which young elementary-age children respond readily.

Pre-adolescent groups (ages nine to thirteen) generally require less use of manipulative materials, but the interaction may benefit from certain activities. These children enjoy small groups composed of members of the same sex and game-activities of interaction and expression. These types of activities allow numerous opportunities for learning and practicing coping behaviors with peers of the same sex and age. Enough time should be scheduled after each activity for members and the leader to discuss behavior elicited during the activity. Participation in the after-activity counseling group must be on a volunteer basis, of course, and the purpose of the discussion must be made clear to members.

Children during the early childhood and pre-adolescent ages need adult models after which to pattern their lives, and this obviously has application to group counseling in elementary schools. The leader provides a model, whether of the same or the opposite sex. Part of the content of these groups should be to bring into awareness the process and importance of modeling.

Leaders who work with elementary school groups find that they must do more "teaching," through a direct approach, of listening skills, membership skills, and individual behaviors than would be necessary or desirable in older age groups. Children need a great deal of help in labeling emotions, as well as in articulating their value systems. Positive emotional development in children is analogous to self-actualization in adults

(Tillinghast, 1970), and leaders of elementary school counseling groups can make provision through the group process to enable children to experience joy as something valuable in itself.

A Consideration of Communication Patterns

Group leaders who work from an existentialist framework and with the extensional model find that the principles and procedures of enhancing communication, as advanced in this book, are appropriate when working with groups of all ages. Children of elementary school age, however, have limitations in communication. They are not practiced at verbalizing feelings as older students are. And even more than older students, they tend to respond with "it" type comments — i.e., facts, events, things away from the group that deal with the there and then. They also tend to make "they" responses — i.e., focus on people away from the group, rather than deal with each other. Thus, young students need help in communicating. A leader might be alert to these types of responses and may either model more productive interaction or discuss interaction patterns directly.

Young students usually "chain" at first; they respond to one another's comments with replies that indicate no verbalized recognition of the content of the other's remarks. For example, a group member might state that he had had a bad night's sleep. A chaining response might be, "I just got a new spread for the bed in my room. It's really neat!" This type of response chains to the output but gives the original speaker no indication that his or her comment held meaning for the receiver. Students of all ages, but particularly those of elementary school age, need to be helped to make associative responses, and to give feedback.

In the associative response, the hearer gives some recognition that he or she has heard the speaker but centers the response egocentrically. Taking the group member's comment about his bad night's sleep, the associative responder might reply, "Yeah, I know what you mean. I had a rough night, too. I'm beat today." This type of response leaves the original speaker with some small degree of satisfaction, but he has received only a

203

minimal amount of feedback from the verbalization. He was heard but does not know if he was understood.

A group leader can, through modeling, teach students to give feedback types of responses. These require a high degree of listening skills on the part of students, but this is one of the functions of the group process — to help members learn to listen to each other. The feedback level of response centers on what the speaker is saying, responds to it, and enriches it. In responding to the comment on the bad night's sleep, a feedback response might be, "You seem kind of tired. It's hard to get along without enough sleep." With such responses, the speakers know that they have been heard, that they have been understood, and that their feelings are recognized. All group participants have some difficulty in learning to give this sort of feedback, but elementary school students have a particular struggle in learning how to communicate at a level in which they transmit "hearing" feelings and unverbalized messages.

ELEMENTARY SCHOOL CLASSROOM GROUPS

So far in this book we have discussed the extensional group model as it pertains to counseling. Temporarily removing children from the normal classroom routine to specifically attend to a special issue or problem — e.g., Blaker and Bennett's (1970) group counseling with shy elementary-aged children — is consistent with *counseling*. The authors would like to extend the concept of "group" to include more natural, informal group situations, such as the classroom.

School children spend a lot of their time in groups of some kind as part of their educational experience. In the classroom setting, group activities tend to be highly structured as compared with other types of group settings. The teacher is usually the primary influence on the content of discussion and controls the directions taken by the group. The authors believe that classroom group leaders (teachers) can utilize certain elements of the extensional model to be more effective in performing their duties. The authors hasten to emphasize that we are proposing the extensional model as an *adjunct* to the traditional role of the teacher, and certainly not as a replacement of any existing educational model.

The following anecdote is taken from a primary school classroom where the teacher periodically introduced extensional group-type activities to help the students learn to interact more openly and honestly with each other.

The children had just returned from morning recess and were seating themselves in a circle. The teacher asked for those who had had a good time to raise their hands. Most of the hands shot up, but a few children apparently had not had a good time. The teacher suggested that the class play an "I Appreciate/I Resent" game. Several "I appreciate" statements were offered by children who had enjoyed themselves. Meanwhile, Matthew's long face obviously conveyed that if he were to say something, it would be an "I resent" message. With the teacher's encouragement, Matthew finally spoke to her.

Matthew: *(With a scowl)* Miss A., I resent Tommy for pushing me down and getting my new pants wet.

Teacher: Can you say that directly to Tommy?

Matthew moved over to where he could look Tommy right in the eye. As he began to repeat his "I resent" message, a slight smile began to appear on his face.

Teacher: Matthew, feel your face. What's it doing?

Matthew: *(Patting his face and mouth with increasing glee)* It's smiling!

Teacher: Is that a "resent" face?

Matthew: Nope.

Teacher:	Then, let's see . . . should you change your face to match the "resent" or should you change "resent" to match your face? What would you like to tell Tommy?
Matthew:	*(Thinking for a moment, refocusing on Tommy's face, and then, with a beaming smile)* Tommy, I appreciate you pushing me down and getting my new pants wet.

With that, the two little boys locked arms around each other's shoulders and remained that way until the group was concluded.

We all tend to overlook much of the potential for communication and positive interaction. Unfortunately, teachers often get caught in a pattern of noticing primarily negative things that take place in classes. Extensional group activities might be helpful in refocusing teacher attention on positive student interaction.

Some of the typical goals of classroom group activities are:

> achieving a curriculum or instructional goal
> helping new students get acquainted
> problem solving
> demonstrating democratic principles
> increasing confidence to participate in discussions
> clarifying values.

When students enter a newly formed class, they wonder, "What's this teacher going to be like?" "What are my classmates going to be like?" "Are they going to be smart? Tough? Friendly?" Unfortunately, teachers are often unconcerned about their students' personal uncertainties and curiosities about their class members. It would take very little time away from instructional objectives for a teacher, using an extensional approach, to attend to these natural concerns of students.

Whether by design or chance, every classroom develops its own unique micro-society. Through interaction that is mostly informal and unplanned, a "pecking order" emerges among students. Leadership roles are informally identified, group values are formed, and protocols of behavior are established, which are as distinctive as they are implicit. Such micro-societies are inevitable in any classroom. Teachers sometimes overlook the fact that these micro-societies have an important influence on students' achievement and attitudes. The influence can be positive or negative, and even when a teacher is aware of the class social structure, he or she may be uncertain about what to do to contribute to its healthy development. We are convinced that extensional group-type activities can serve as a vehicle for influencing the positive development of the classroom's micro-society, and thus improve its educational and emotional climate.

The statement above is based on two assumptions: First, the authors assume that students learn more efficiently when they are personally involved in the learning process. Second, we assume that peers are extremely influential in affecting student attitudes and behaviors. When students can be accepting of themselves, they are more likely to be accepting of others. Only when they function well within their peer group will they be able to attain the utmost of their potentials. We would expect, therefore, greater achievement with comparatively less effort in an educational environment where positive interaction among peers is built into the curriculum, and where students are encouraged to explore and examine their feelings about themselves, their classmates, and their educational experiences.

The importance of the realness and authenticity of the leader-teacher deserves emphasis. Often, teachers function as they think teachers *ought* to function, denying themselves expression of their humanness. Teachers *are* human, not robots, yet the traditionally prescribed role of a teacher seems to focus on analyses and facts, ignoring human feeling. Relinquishing facades and prescribed role expectancies is necessary if an atmosphere of spontaneity, freedom, and trust is to be created. In this kind of atmosphere, the teacher and student are in touch with each other as co-human beings, rather than as a superior and subordinate.

Historically, teachers have ignored or neglected the educational importance of considering students' feelings. During the late 1960s and 1970s an increasing number of theoretical models and programs in the affective domain, paralleling the extensional group model, were devised for instruction. This emerging interest in affective education is long overdue. When we conceptualize learning in the cognitive, psychomotor, and affective domains, most educators are uncertain about what they are supposed to do in the affective domain. Their own education usually did not attend to this area, and it is difficult to operate in unfamiliar territory.

RESOURCES FOR ELEMENTARY SCHOOL COUNSELING AND CLASSROOM GROUPS

A number of resource materials may prove useful when working with elementary school-age children. The annotated presentation below is merely representative of the kinds of resources available. The reader is urged to contact the bibliographic source for the original materials if interested in further information.

Elementary School Counseling Group Resources

Although the literature specifically addressed to elementary school group counselors is limited in comparison with the literature focusing on other educational groups, several approaches described below might be of interest to leaders who plan on working with students of this age and situation. The first, a handbook issued by the Los Angeles Unified School District, is specifically aimed at pupil personnel workers who deal with elementary school counseling groups. The second is a behavioral approach to group counseling with children, followed by an existential, here-and-now approach. A discussion of an activity group approach is followed by a model that considers the group process as a means of developing each student's potential.

A Guide to Group Counseling in Elementary Schools

The Los Angeles Unified School District (1969) developed a useful publication for elementary school group counselors. In this handbook, group counseling is viewed as a means to alleviate anxieties and emotional tensions, to resolve conflicts, to develop self-understanding, to facilitate the learning of acceptable, gratifying behavior, to assist in achieving maturity and increased sensitivity to the needs of others, and to help each student evaluate his or her own behavior. Suggestions concerning group interaction are followed by a discussion on how and when to terminate a group, and evaluation methodology as it applies to the group counseling program.

Cognitive-Behavioral Approach
to Group Counseling with Children

This approach was conceived by Mayer, Rohen, and Whitley (1969) for counseling with elementary school children. It is based on a combination of dissonance theory and social learning theory. Mayer believes that group counseling offers an excellent environment for the creation of dissonance, since more than one model is provided for each student to listen to, observe, and interact with. Thus, contradictory items of information are likely to be available in the group. Positive reinforcement can be supplied both by group members and the leader.

A Reality Here-and-Now Approach

Bigelow and Thorne (1969) compared two elementary school counseling groups, using the Hill Interaction Matrix as the instrumentation. The research design contrasted a group in which the leader attempted to work at the Confrontation level on the HIM (Hill, 1971) with a group in which the leader assumed a nondirective stance. There were six sessions. The group that received little leader intervention interacted at a significantly lower therapeutic level than did the confrontive group. At the end of the six sessions, the group that focused on Hill's more productive level (Confrontation) showed significantly more productive interactions.

Activity Group Counseling

Another approach to group counseling with elementary school children was suggested by Charles King (1957). His approach is geared to students between the ages of eight and fourteen, working in a group of the same sex and numbering from five to eight. King's comments are addressed to groups that meet outside the public school setting, but his procedures could be adapted to the school situation. The "club" (group) meets in a room designed to permit a maximum range of physical activity — running, jumping, and chasing — but also makes provision for "retiring" corners. A round table and several smaller tables are essential, as are tools and materials consisting of "easy" arts and crafts resources.

King emphasized that the thing produced in the club is never permitted to be an end in itself; rather, the process of creating and the emotional experiences of the process are the objective of the activity. Food is considered essential, as one of the strongest bonds in creating a sense of belonging in a group. The leader assumes a neutral and accepting role, but he or she provides a point of reality and reassuring authority to the group. The leader does not talk much, hands group decisions back to the group wherever feasible, but is always available.

King's activity group approach is almost totally noninterpretive; he sees the force of the process as lying in the dynamic acting-out between members of the group around the stable fulcrum of the leader. The activity group is aimed at enhancing, encouraging, and strengthening self-esteem, role-identification, and a capacity for relationships, both with peers and with adults.

Developing Human Potential

Otto (1970) has maintained consistently that "every student is a gifted student," and his suggestions for developing the elementary school student's potential embrace an appropriate approach to group counseling with students of this age. Otto's stance is "life-affirmative." He stated: "Man is a continuous process of self-creation; Growth in life occurs through human relationship; Self-knowledge is the first step toward self-realization; Crisis is an opportunity for growth; Humor is the confident expression of a developing selfhood; The optimal use of communication is a requisite in developing human potential" (pp. 133-166).

Otto feels strongly that, for an elementary pupil's potential to be enhanced, it is necessary to provide personal growth experiences for the teacher, who will then be more aware of the student's needs and will have greater ability to respond to these needs. Emphasizing strengths cannot be too strongly recommended to leaders who are working with groups of students in the public school setting — particularly in the elementary school setting.

Elementary School Classroom Discussion Group Resources

As mentioned earlier, the authors are convinced that *group* work should be considered in a broader context than just counseling — e.g., teaching and guidance groups. Classroom teachers who are unaware of the group dynamics occurring among their students are inadequately trained. The distinction between group counseling and classroom group discussion is sometimes obscure. Their purposes differ, and *counseling* usually calls for a departure from the normal classroom routine. But the process of interpersonal contact, speaking spontaneously in the here and now, and receiving feedback is just as important to a skilled teacher as it is to a skilled group leader. Both of them are, in reality, group facilitators. Whereas group leaders may focus *entirely* on the interactive process of the group participants, classroom teachers call upon their awareness and group

211

leadership functions at times when they think their students' learning can be positively effected.

Most of the structured activities referred to below could be adapted for use in group counseling. Owing to the authors' commitment to expanding the extensional group model for more general use, we have decided to present the following catalytic suggestions in this section. The only reason these catalysts do not appear in Chapter 8 is that their design calls for a relatively high degree of structure, certain materials, and pre-planning suitable particularly to elementary-age children.

Dimensions in Personality

Pflaum/Standard, Inc. offers an exciting series of books and audiovisual materials for elementary school children, grades 1 through 6. For example, to learn about dealing with anger, students are shown a large cartoon of a mean-looking gorilla and are asked, "Have you ever felt like this gorilla looks? Walk and roar like a gorilla. Don't forget to pound your chest." They are encouraged to talk about what prompts "gorilla" types of feelings. Shortly afterward, the children are to focus on their teacher and ask, "Do you think your teacher has ever felt like this gorilla?" The point of the program is to help children recognize that feelings are natural and belong to everyone. How we cope with our feelings can have disastrous or beneficial results.

The materials for older elementary school children explore values clarification, self-identification, and self-acceptance. *Here I am* (Limbacker, 1969) and *I Am Not Alone* (Limbacker, 1970) exemplify the nature of Pflaum/Standard *Dimensions* programs for older elementary school children.

Magic Circle

The Institute for Personal Effectiveness in Children pub-lishes materials and curriculum guides that were originally developed by Harold Bessell and Uvaldo Palomares (Bessell,

1968; Bessell & Palomares, 1970). The group discussion/process (e.g., the "Magic Circle") is structured in such a way as to progress systematically through various stages of self-observation, self-awareness, a commitment to improving oneself, and to improving interpersonal skills.

DUSO (Developing Understanding of Self and Others)

Dinkmeyer (1973) created the DUSO program for helping primary-aged (grades K-3) children express their feelings, fears, and concerns. Along with other media and materials, hand puppets are marvelous catalytic devices for helping children express their feelings. They can talk *to* the puppet, or the puppet can speak *for* the child (who is manipulating it). This is an excellent program for helping teach very young children to interact and express their thoughts and feelings.

Handbook of Personal Growth Activities for the Classroom

Robert and Isabel Hawley (1972) have compiled activities intended to stimulate classroom discussions in the areas of self-identification, values clarification, and interpersonal communication for elementary school children. Their activities are described in such a way that the teacher knows exactly what objective (e.g., children are to decide their own grade) and what equipment (e.g., chalkboard, pencil, butcher paper) is required to complete the activity.

Pow-Wow

Muro and Dinkmeyer (1977) have devised a systematic way of allowing children a way to express themselves and take responsibility for their actions. A "pow-wow," which may occur while other children are working at their seats or in reading groups, for example, involves a small (four- to six-member)

213

group of children in a three-step process. First, they are asked to express something positive about themselves, others, or their educational experience. Second, they are to state what goals they intend to pursue for making themselves better persons. The group is encouraged to contribute impressions as to whether the expressed goals are realistic. Third, "gripes," if any, are invited about the classroom, the teacher, classmates — *anything* that seems to be an irritant or detraction from the child's learning experience.

One could ask, "What if there is a room full of 'gripers'?" In our experience with group work and methods similar to this, the encouragement to express negative feelings usually gives a realistic perspective to the "griper's" concerns. An invitation for individuals to express openly what has been covertly troubling them most often takes the sting out of irrational or vindictive concerns. The beauty of "pow-wow" is the encouragement of *full* affective expression and the commitment for doing something about the children's happiness or unhappiness.

The Other Side of the Report Card

Larry Chase's *The Other Side of the Report Card: A How-To-Do-It Program for Affective Education* (1975) is a delightful book on how teachers can work with elementary school children to develop their sense of awareness and interpersonal skills. Chase's approach is a bit more academically oriented than the references previously mentioned. He precedes activities and exercises, many of which include reading and writing effort on the part of students, with clear educational objectives. This book includes an extensive bibliography of printed materials and audio-visual aids for teachers to use with their students.

One Hundred Ways for Improving Self-Concept

Canfield and Wells (1976) compiled this excellent collection of activities for teachers and parents to use with young children.

The book is a *must* for anyone who desires to expand children's affective education and interpersonal skills. It is an invaluable resource.

Values Clarification

The Simon, Howe, and Kirschenbaum manual, *Values Clarification* (1972) is perhaps the best-known resource of its kind. It is not intended specifically for stimulating group interaction, but the strategies presented certainly could not be implemented without group interaction. Like several resources already mentioned, this manual was originally intended for young children. Creative group leaders/teachers should have little difficulty in adapting and modifying many of the activities for students and group participants of any age. The authors have used activities from *Values Clarification* with age groups ranging from elementary through high school levels, in college, and with senior citizen groups.

A Human Development Process for Educational Systems (TRIBES)

Jeanne Gibbs and Andre Allen (1978), professional educators, wrote this process for educators who wish to add an affective dimension to their curriculum, grades K-12. TRIBES is one of the most imaginative and comprehensive educational program the authors have encountered. Instructional objectives, suggested activities, and detailed guidelines for using the materials are included. The structure of TRIBES is helpful to teachers and group leaders who are using it as a new approach. The materials, however, are not so rigid as to discourage adaptiveness. Although TRIBES does not mention the extensional group model, the two concepts are totally compatible, and the authors recommend TRIBES as a means of helping students, K-12, interact in a positive, constructive manner. TRIBES may not yet be as well known as *Values Clarification*, but it has much more to offer.

HIGH SCHOOL GROUP COUNSELING

Adolescence is a period when young people eagerly experiment with adult behavior and attitudes while gradually relinquishing the securities of childhood. It is an exciting, yet, at times, frightening period of growth for many teenagers. Adults who attempt to advise and counsel young people through this transition period are often more impressed with the wisdom of their guidance than are the recipients. The values and experience gap between adults and adolescents can be sizable and, as a result, frustrating to adults who are genuinely trying to be of help. Nevertheless, it is no less frustrating and confusing to teenagers who are seeking a sense of self-identification in which they feel competent, independent, and accepted among peers. This is a common adolescent concern, although the intensity of the concerns and confusion varies considerably. Adolescents are most likely to turn to their peers in search of answers and support. In their bid for independence and self-identification, most teens are particularly conscious of the peer-relevant mores and values that are in vogue.

Acceptance by peers is significantly more important to high school students than are the opinions and advice of adults. Among adolescents, what is acceptable and unacceptable by teen standards is known by all, constructed and imposed by the students themselves. Simply stated, students decide that some aspects of their existence are "safe" to share. Other interests, thoughts, and aspirations that they might genuinely wish to share are not because students suspect they would be ridiculed or rejected by volunteering them.

For example, a contemporary pastime that seems to be socially acceptable to high school students is motorcycling. Therefore, it would definitely be okay to describe oneself as a motorcycle enthusiast. A greater risk would be involved in announcing a deep involvement with Scouting and an aspiration to Eagle Scout status. Probably some "clown" in the group will exclaim derisively, "Boy Scouts!"

Involvement in sports — almost any variety of sporting activity — is preferable to and "safer" than speaking with pride about beekeeping. Sharing the excitement of a weekend party is less risky than describing the excitement of a book read over the weekend.

In many classrooms peer influence can develop an insidious character. For whatever reasons, some students are judged by their peers to be not "with it" by contemporary peer standards. Even if these individuals are not patently ostracized, they are often intentionally "not noticed."

As mentioned earlier in this chapter, students spend a good part of their school day in some form of group activity — committees, task-oriented classroom groups, and so on. Most often, though, group interaction takes place in casual gatherings in the classroom, corridors, cafeteria, and after school.

We have already proposed that group interaction offers the potential for growth and positive change, and since young people are in groups anyway, why doesn't this potential emerge naturally? One of the basic reasons why it does not emerge naturally is that teenagers typically are beginning to monitor their behavior, how they dress, what they say, and so forth. The proclivity toward fads and conformity is probably the most obvious verification that teens (all of us, for that matter) are concerned, to varying degrees, about how we are perceived by others. In their peer consciousness, teens are beginning to manifest certain "D"-level characteristics to protect themselves from possible peer rejection. In high school, students with a weak self-identity or poor self-concept typically are concerned about behaving as they think they *ought* to, rather than as they are. Consider the following anecdote.

Three high school boys were observed walking down the street. They were all dressed identically in Levis, T-shirts and dark windbreakers. Their manner of dress, the way they walked with their hands shoved deep in their front pockets, and their hunched shoulders identified them as "tough" or "cool." They seemed quite conscious of their image and took care to talk and look "cool."

As they crossed the street, one of the boys tripped on the curb and fell to the sidewalk. His two companions both looked at him, not knowing whether to be concerned or to laugh at him. It was as if they were waiting to see his reaction before expressing their own. Without any outward signs of embarrassment or loss of control, and *without taking his hands out of his pockets,* he bounced up in a flash and proceeded with his friends, who had hardly broken stride. They moved on as if nothing had happened, walking and looking "cool."

Most "normal" people would have displayed embarrassment, but the young man in the illustration above apparently felt he would have risked a lot to dress differently, walk differently, be "cool" differently, or to *be himself.* In some mysterious manner, dress, behavior, and attitude acquire an almost prescriptive character among teens. Protecting facades seems as important to teens as to adults. Many high school students have difficulty revealing themselves authentically, and often what looks spontaneous is really a facade of being peppy and sharp. Other students appear bored and sullen because that is the image they wish to convey.

The authors are convinced that young people have serious thoughts and concerns that they would really like to communicate to others. Unfortunately, educational settings do not allow many opportunities for encouraging this type of interaction. Adolescents' natural strengths and resources can be channeled and shared for mutual benefit if a sensitive and knowledgeable adult (group leader — teacher — counselor) is available to facilitate interaction. Since peer influence is such a pervasive force among teens, why not capitalize on its power for constructive purposes? The school climate and instructional efficiency would be improved immensely if such opportunities were made available.

We have concluded that the abilities of teachers and counselors might best be utilized in structuring group situations in which students can share their opinions and perceptions. This may lead to confrontation between students or between students and teachers, but confrontation can be constructive. Frequently, a peer confrontation includes the same information with which an adult might confront the student. The main difference is the identity of the confronter. Our hypothesis is simple: It is more difficult for an adolescent to reject or deny the opinions of a peer than those of an adult. The feelings expressed by peers seem to have more impact.

The following examples should indicate the importance of peer interaction. Imagine, if you will, the following statements being made to adolescents by an adult. On the other hand, imagine the same interaction between adolescents.

"I really think you have a lot to be proud of. You're attractive and intelligent."

"You don't bore me. I think you have had many interesting experiences."

"I think you're blowing it. You look strung out all the time."

"You always act so hard. You don't need to act that way. I don't think you are really that way at all."

"You look cheap."

"You seem to genuinely care about other people. I admire that."

These examples are excerpted from student comments made in actual high school group counseling situations. As concerned adults, we possibly would have liked to have made these same statements to young people on occasion. If teachers were to say the same things to students, however, the statements would probably be rejected as being "your values, not mine." If a student makes the same kind of statement to another student, we think it stands a better chance of being heard and considered.

Consequently, the group leader should try to develop and maintain an environment designed to maximize listening and assimilation of the information and opinions being shared among adolescents.

The extensional group model seems to be an ideal vehicle for focusing on interaction that is honest, spontaneous, and positive. The group leader does not prohibit feedback that is negative or calculated, but he or she is careful not to permit continued negative feedback intended to be destructive or vindictive. A leader can use negative feedback in the group process to influence authentic, positive interaction. Extensional group techniques, however, are not designed or employed for evoking negative confrontations. Our approach to the group process centers on capitalizing on positive feedback.

Before the start of a high school group counseling project, notices were sent home to parents explaining what was to happen. A parent called the counselor to inquire, "What's wrong with my son? Why should he be asked to be counseled in a group?" The counselor replied, "We're inviting your son to participate because there is something he can contribute to the group. The reason he was invited to join wasn't because there is something wrong with him!"

This illustrates the authors' positive approach to group work. Our assumption is that learning and personal growth are maximized when we feel good about ourselves and when we have confidence in the support and acknowledgment of our peers.

Organizing Group Counseling in High Schools

Educational goals that can be achieved through the use of group counseling in public schools are a legitimate concern of school counselors. Bates (1968) conducted research to identify which of those goals could be achieved through group processes when working with adolescents in a high school setting. According to her study, group counseling could be used to help students become more receptive to the learning process through a reduction of tensions and hostilities. In one of the group formats of this study, students were helped to maintain a grade-point average, improve behaviors in the classroom, demonstrate more applied effort, and increase daily attendance. Students in the groups expanded the occupational choices into which they projected themselves, and these chosen occupations were more realistic when assessed against the students' academic potential. Group participants came to feel they were of more value to themselves, were more self-accepting, and were more aware of themselves as unique persons. They also came to place more value on others and become more aware of the universality of human experiences.

The goals and objectives that can be achieved through group counseling are consonant with the goals and objectives of education. In the extensional model, group leaders assist prospective group members in identifying the goals and objectives that each wishes to achieve. The leader's responsibility is to be knowledgable about group research and adolescent development, so that he or she can help members identify achievable, realistic objectives.

Staff Preparation

The typical high school probably misunderstands the purpose of group to a greater extent than does any other institution. Counselors who wish to initiate group counseling will likely find their time in staff preparation well spent. Without the staff's understanding and support, almost any group counseling program will encounter difficulty.

First of all, the administrators' support *must* be obtained — not just permission, but support, preferably enthusiastic support. If an administrator gives only lukewarm agreement, counselors may want to delay the group counseling program until they are able to elicit clearer understandings on the part of administrators of the educational advantages of a group counseling program.

After the support of the administration has been gained, a general presentation concerning the nature of group counseling, its values and educational components, should be made to the faculty. At this point, it is recommended that the building administrator express support of the group counseling program to the entire faculty.

Selection of Students

The best group member is a self-referred group member; group counseling should be optional for participants. Leaders will find that after a program of group counseling has been carried on for a semester or so, students will voluntarily request group counseling. Until they are familiar with the experience, however, the leader may have to arrange some orientation directed at the entire student body. The leader may go to classrooms and contact all students through a general guidance presentation, such as that provided in Appendix C. Students should not be asked to volunteer for counseling groups at the time of the group guidance presentation. Rather, the leader should suggest that students who are interested see him or her personally.

Once the leader has eight to twelve students who wish to be in a group, the organization can begin. The authors believe that homogeneous groups are a myth, and that organizing a group around some "common problem" is not functional. All group members are homogeneous in that they are all unique human beings, each an individual unlike any other individual who has ever lived or ever will live. The notion that a group with "attendance problems" or "behavior problems" has a common problem is most likely erroneous. If a school has labeled eight students as having "attendance problems," the etiology of the attendance problem of each of the eight will probably be quite different. *Groups organized around a school problem are appropriately guidance groups, and leaders should never use them to seduce students into becoming counseling groups.*

The authors suggest that beginning leaders restrict group membership to students of not more than two grade levels. Group progress may be hampered if students are too divergent in age or development. Another suggestion is that beginning group leaders work with students of one sex for their first group, because such a group is easier to handle. Coeducational groups are preferred once the leader gains experience. In composing a counseling group, leaders should take into consideration the degree to which each of the participants is verbal; too few or too many highly verbal members may inhibit group interaction.

Number of Sessions

The school-based extensional group model suggests that leaders schedule a pre-group interview, eight group counseling sessions, and a post-group interview. Thus, a counseling group can be organized, conducted, and evaluated within the framework of a school quarter. If the pre-group interview is done well, and if the group leaders are skilled, eight sessions should be sufficiently productive. The notion of continuing one group for a semester or a year (or two!) in the public school setting is neither necessary nor desirable.

If a leader believes an individual group member should continue working in a group, the member can be reassigned, and thus not be denied the opportunity for continuance. At the same time, each of the group members will have had the experience of working with a limited number of sessions and may have internalized a basic fact of living — that opportunities (and life) have limits.

Logistics

If possible, a group should meet in other than a classroom setting. Privacy should be maximum, with *no* interruptions permitted. Chairs should be arranged in a circle but not around a table, since nonverbal communication involves the entire body.

The leader must begin on time, even if only one member is present. The session also must end on time. Beginning group leaders tend to want to extend the time of their sessions, as groups led by beginners characteristically get down to work toward the end of a session. If neophyte leaders allow the time to be extended, they are denying group members the opportunity to learn limits, and therefore to gain experience in reality testing.

Usually the group meets weekly for one class period. Meeting for the same period each week is best, but if the group leader works in a traditionally scheduled school, he or she may elect to rotate the periods for group meetings (e.g., first period first week, second period second week, etc.). In a modular scheduled school, groups can meet when the student has free time, but we suggest that no groups be organized before or after school or during the lunch hour. If counseling is a legitimate part of the educational program, time ought to be available for group counseling as well as classroom instruction.

Checksheet

The checklist below (Figure 9.1) for organizing the group might be useful as a quick reference.

FIGURE 9.1
Checksheet For Organizing a Counseling Group In Schools

	Yes	No
1. Did you clear with administration and faculty?	____	____
2. Have you selected from eight to twelve potential members?	____	____
3. Have you made a general presentation to students in the classroom setting? (optional)	____	____
4. If this is your first group, are they all one sex?	____	____
5. Is the age span no more than two years among students?	____	____

224

6. Did you interview each one individually? ⸻ ⸻

7. Were you and each group member able to specify objectives in the pre-group interview? ⸻ ⸻

8. Did you clearly explain each counselee's membership responsibility? ⸻ ⸻

9. Did you locate some place in which to meet where you will have uninterrupted privacy? ⸻ ⸻

10. Did you clearly communicate time limits and number of sessions? ⸻ ⸻

11. Have you planned a post-group session with individual members to discuss their objectives? ⸻ ⸻

Selected Group Format

Each group member is unique. Each group leader is unique. The extraordinary qualities of individual members and individual leaders make each group unpredictable to some degree. The complexities that comprise the entity called "group" are so intricate that they defy definition and, therefore, anticipation. Experienced and inexperienced leaders alike approach each group as an unknown. Perhaps a major difference between experienced leaders and inexperienced leaders is that the former know they can never be sure what will evolve in a group and the latter still believe that, in time, they might.

The suggestions that follow, therefore, are presented as a skeletal framework to which the leaders must give the substance of life. Variations are infinite. The format advanced below is only a benchmark, only the sketch of an outline. The intent is to provide a simplistic reference point from which leaders can move creatively into the intricacies of the group process.

Group Counseling with Pre-group Interview. The group leader makes a group guidance presentation in classroom, using the pamphlet *So You Are Going To Be in Group Counseling* (see Appendix C). It covers responsibilities of group membership,

225

limits of the group, such as number of sessions, size, areas to be explored, and what members *might* get out of the experience. The leader may wish to discuss the Johari Window. The leader asks students who wish to join a counseling group to see him or her in his or her office. The leader avoids using group pressure to stimulate individual interest, does not ask students to indicate an interest in joining a counseling group while making the group guidance presentation.

Leaders should (1) Obtain group leadership skills; (2) Consult with administration, informing them of procedures, objectives, and benefits of the group counseling program; and (3) With the support of administration, inform faculty and, if possible, parents and school board members.

Leaders should then observe the following procedure: (1) Conduct pre-group individual interview with selected participants. (Those who cannot be placed in a group at this time are contacted and placed on a "wait" list.) Identify individual objectives and write them on 3" x 5" cards; (2) Hold eight sessions — one class period each, with each session "capped"; (3) Conduct post-group interview to assess objectives. (The leader should not make implications that gains made should be the same as objectives set at the group's beginning.); (4) If the leader believes a member needs to continue, offer to place him or her in another group.

Catalytic techniques. Specific activities that could be used include the following (refer to Chapter 8 for descriptions):

Session 1: Use mild confrontation technique, such as "Pair and Share."

Session 2: Perhaps use "New Names" or "Symbolic Objects" to begin interaction — respond to values, priorities, concepts of self.

Session 3: Maybe utilize no catalytic technique; group may begin self, and leaders should avoid having participants become dependent on activities to begin interaction.

Session 4:   Ask if anyone wants to begin or if the group wishes the leader to begin interaction. Possibly use "Magic Shop," "Territoriality," or "Three Adjectives" — low to moderate intensity techniques.

Session 5:   Same as above; if technique is used, consider "Presentation of Self: Clothes" or "Taking a Trip."

Session 6:   If technique is desired, consider "Mirror Image," "First Impressions," etc.

Session 7:   Use a nonverbal technique, if appropriate, or "Strength Bombardment."

Session 8:   Use no technique, or ask members to respond to, "As a group member, I . . ." Tie up loose ends. Be sure to have a "go-around" during this session so each participant has an opportunity to verbalize unfinished business.

These are only suggestions. Leaders can create an endless variety of catalytic techniques.

Special Considerations in High School Counseling Groups

When high school counseling groups begin to acquire the potential for intense interaction of the type that is observed among adult groups, some special concerns arise. Examining long-term values, assuming personal responsibility, planning for the future, understanding sexuality, clarifying self-identification, and getting along with parents and authority figures are issues that do not normally emerge in groups of younger children but are common in adolescent groups.

Because of the potential for "heavy" issues, the group leader should have a clear picture of why group counseling seems appropriate and desirable for his or her particular group of high school students. Being absolutely clear on this point is a requisite for enlisting the support and understanding of the faculty and administration.

Furthermore, many high schools have a policy requiring parent permission for a student's group participation. Sharing informative, printed material that explains group counseling is helpful. (Again, Appendix C provides an example of such material.) This is useful and convenient for informing anyone — students, parents, faculty, administration — who is interested in learning about group counseling. The thought and effort invested in writing printed material about group work sharpen leaders' sense of clarity and purpose concerning their group work.

Although member responsibilities are described in the printed material, adolescents tend to test adults and situations that permit open dialogue about issues that are not normally discussed in school. Therefore, while encouraging group members to be open, spontaneous, and free is important, adolescents sometimes seem to need stronger reminders that freedom to act and speak (in group) must also recognize and respect the rights of others. Confidentiality must be honored by everyone in the group.

Part of the challenge stems from the attitude that some adolescents bring to their group experience. The group leader may have to make a special effort to convince participants that group time is valuable and must be used seriously. The group is not party time. Members will benefit to the extent that they contribute and participate authentically.

A Consideration of Communication Patterns

The range of and gaps in social and communication skills seem more pronounced among adolescents, particularly those in their early teens, than among any other age group. Interaction with members of the opposite sex is often awkward. Preoccupation with status, age, and grade-level differences can interfere with clear and sincere communication. Even sustaining normal eye contact is a problem for some teens. In short, adolescence is a time of relative uncertainty about oneself, demonstrated sometimes by social clumsiness and difficulty with clear, personal articulation.

There are no "special" techniques for group leaders to use with teens having this difficulty, but understanding the developmental and transitory personality aspects of adolescence can guide group leaders in their efforts to help members express themselves openly and to learn from their experience with other teens. The awkwardness observed in many adolescents requires, perhaps, more leader vigilance for encouragement and support than for other types of groups. Patience and perseverance are two indispensable leader qualities for facilitating group interaction among teens.

A communication pattern that lingers from pre-teen days is difficulty with conscious self-disclosing in the here and now and the tendency not to listen to group mates. This statement is a generalization about teens, and adults are certainly not immune to such group behavior. But the pattern seems to be more noticeable among adolescents, partly because of their self-consciousness and partly because schools rarely encourage the kind of interaction that is encouraged in group.

What a teen may intend to be self-disclosure is frequently an impersonal narrative, as if the teen were describing himself or herself as a character in a movie or TV script, through phrases like, "and I go . . .," "and she said . . .," "and then *I* said . . .," "and she goes. . . " Personalizing pronouns as a part of speaking directly about oneself is foreign to most adolescents, as well as to most adults. Instead of saying "I" or "my" when referring to themselves, they tend to detract from the intensity of a personal statement by saying, "you," "it," "we," "us." "Ya know" and "OK?" are examples of "filler-phrases" that mean nothing in themselves but may give speakers the feeling that they have added substance to their statements. These detractions are not used consciously to avoid deeper, more personal interaction; they are speech habits developed over time, probably as a result of earlier modeling among peers. Speech patterns are copied, just as music and clothing styles are copied.

Consider the following statement taken from a group session with high school freshmen:

Paula: . . . and my name comes blaring over the intercom, ya know . . . "Paula C., please report to the vice principal's office . . ." and I go, "Oh, no! (rolling her eyes) Not again!" . . . OK . . . and then, ya know what? The teacher, she goes, "PAULA, did you hear your name?" . . . and I go, "If he wants to see me, why doesn't he come here?" . . . just kidding, ya know . . . and the class cracks up laughing . . . OK . . . Well, she gets mad, ya know, and starts yelling her lungs out . . . ya know.

I mean . . . ya know . . . ya kinda get embarrassed when your name comes blaring over the intercom . . . that's a bummer, ya know . . . cheez, everybody in school knows you're in trouble . . . ya know . . . and then, having this teacher screaming like a banshee . . . ya know . . . and it was just a little joke . . . OK. It's like a prison around here . . . OK . . . and the teachers are like guards . . . ya know.

Throughout the statement above, the student is really talking about *her* experience. The leader's task in extensional group is to help Paula focus on speaking personally and to distinguish between the description of an historical event and the feelings she might be experiencing about it in the *present*.

Another communication pattern to which all groups are subject, but one that is particularly noticeable in pre-teen and teen groups, is the tendency not to really listen to each other. They may *hear* the words spoken by another, but they do not understand or empathize. For example, in the statement above, while Paula is talking about her experience, nonlisteners are recalling when they got called to the vice principal's office, and if they respond in the group they will likely narrate their experiences. "Story telling" is a common communication pattern in adolescent groups, and a leader must work to rechannel it to more productive here-and-now interaction. "Story telling" is never a here-and-now expression.

HIGH SCHOOL CLASSROOM GROUPS

Most high school teachers encourage discussions and comparing and sharing of ideas and opinions, but few make an effort to teach students how to improve their abilities to interact constructively with each other. Ideally, students should be learning to listen to each other with a reasonable degree of respect and courtesy. This ideal is often taken for granted.

The assumptions and educational goals discussed in the "elementary school classroom groups" section of this chapter are essentially the same for high school classroom groups. Adaptation for age, grade level, and maturity are obviously important; other considerations need not be repeated.

RESOURCES FOR HIGH SCHOOL COUNSELING AND CLASSROOM GROUPS

As already mentioned, high school counseling groups seem to be closer in character to adult groups and rely more on spontaneous interaction than do younger age groups. Chapter 8 is our primary catalytic resource for adolescent group counseling.

The distinction between group guidance and classroom discussion groups is murky and, perhaps, not even important to clarify beyond their distinctive goals and objectives. In practice, both guidance and classroom discussion groups would use the extensional group model as we have already described. The point of the model is to attempt to stimulate honest, spontaneous, and personally relevant interaction among students.

The annotated list of resources presented below is purposefully brief and is intended to supplement the resources suggested in Chapter 8. Some of the resources listed in the elementary school section (e.g., TRIBES) are appropriate for high school use when adapted, but the resources listed below are not appropriate for elementary school use.

Nothing Never Happens. Johnson et al. (1974) have developed a marvelous interpersonal psychology curriculum for high school students. A well-conceived and informative teacher's manual accompanies the student text. The manual provides activities that do not appear in the text. This allows for flexibility and adaptiveness when the teacher thinks an activity in the students' text is not suitable for the moment. Considerable attention is devoted to problems of semantics, group interaction, and leadership. A "discovery" method of learning is encouraged through the use of "triggers" (structured activities similar to our "catalysts"). Triggers are intended to stimulate interpersonal contact, which is then encouraged to become more natural and spontaneous.

The 30+ concise journal articles in the back of the teacher's manual cover most of the concepts in interpersonal psychology and self-actualization. Teachers lacking psychological background should be able to develop a reasonably good foundation in this particular area of psychology if they complete all the readings in the teacher's manual.

Self-Awareness Through Group Dynamics. Richard Reichert's (1970) small book has served as a supplement to curricula in several different subject areas. Each chapter briefly presents a different topic, provides open-ended questions for stimulating class discussion, and suggests an activity for experiential learning. Freedom and Responsibility, Prejudice, The Clash of Individual Freedoms, and The Generation Gap are samples of topics included.

Decisions and Outcomes. Originally designed to be a guidance tool, this book by Gelatt et al. (1973) offers an interesting combination of activities for self-exploration and interpersonal discussion. Students focus on values clarification, data collecting, and risk taking — all prerequisite for sensible decision making about one's life. The topics are carefully sequenced for building comprehension. Gelatt and colleagues have taken some rather complex notions (e.g., probability theory) and presented them in a practical, digestible, and personally meaningful way.

232

GROUPS FOR SCHOOL ADMINISTRATORS, FACULTY, AND SUPPORT STAFF

The extensional group model has served well for improving interpersonal contact among the people who operate schools. As most educators know, a sense of isolation is an easy pattern to fall into. Something in the organization and structure of educational settings tends toward isolation. Perhaps it is the closed doors that go with classrooms in session and the business of administration, but isolation tends to breed distrust, and distrust tends to feed the sense of isolation. Without individual and collective attention to this phenomenon, schools can become an unpleasant, lonely place in which to work. Dissonance among faculty, staff, and administration, because of poor communication and misunderstanding, is common. Support staff members, such as secretaries, cafeteria workers, and custodians, also experience isolation, which can be corrected if an effort is made to help people communicate and get to know each other on an open, honest, and humane level.

In an effort to break down this sense of isolation, real or imagined, the entire administration, faculty, and support staff of a large high school was invited to participate in a "communications workshop" consisting of eight two-hour weekly sessions held after school. From among those who indicated their interest, groups of approximately 20 people were organized so that a cross-section of school personnel was represented in each group. In one of the groups, for example, a vice principal, the principal's secretary, a counselor, a part-time counselor's clerk, several teachers from various disciplines, teacher aides, and a cafeteria worker provided an interesting mix of people. The extensional group model was applied, using catalytic activities as primers for discussion. As discussion became more natural and spontaneous, the catalysts were gradually deleted.

The interaction offered some keen insights to several of the participants as to how they were being perceived by their co-workers. The principal's secretary, for example, had no conception of the power and status afforded her by faculty and staff. A cafeteria worker who had felt isolated and unappreciated

233

learned that her steadiness and cheerfulness in the "crunch" of mealtime pressures had been noticed and admired by several people for a long time. The chairman of a large academic department admitted to the strain of being a "boss." He was surprised to be informed that many of his colleagues viewed him as officious and sometimes dictatorial. Because that was not the way that he wanted to be seen, he eagerly sought the advice of his colleagues to help him improve his leadership style.

An encounter between two teachers who had been teaching in adjacent classrooms for several years was touching. Each teacher had thought of the other as being "polished" and sophisticated, but neither had shared these perceptions. As they became better acquainted, they discovered that both had grown up in impoverished neighborhoods where survival was paramount. Both of them had worked their way through college, and both were the only "educated" persons in their families. The shared similarities of their backgrounds, particularly in light of their original misperceptions of each other, marked the beginning of a valued relationship.

The group project was sufficiently successful to be introduced in another of the district's high schools the following year. More than 65 percent of the administration, faculty, and staff completed the communications workshops. The follow-up evaluation revealed that most participants believed that the openness, caring, and trust experienced in the group had generalized to other areas of the school's operations. The entire project was voluntary, although the fact that the administrators were among the first to volunteer may have served as a model. There was no intended pressure on anyone to participate, and most of the evaluation respondents reported that their interest in the workshops was the result of positive comments that had emanated from people who attended the workshops the previous year.

SUMMARY

Educators can be expected to object to using valuable educational time to encourage students to get to know each other and themselves better, particularly if the catalytic activities that are a part of the extensional group process are perceived as "games." Nevertheless, the authors believe that a great deal more learning can take place when students' mental and physical faculties are stimulated. Students are more willing to become involved with the learning process if their spirits and interests are lifted. Becoming involved in mutual sharing will do that.

The important aspect of the extensional group model is that teachers can instigate it, can be involved in the activity themselves, and can control it for educational purposes. This seems far more constructive than the spontaneous activities that erupt from students who are bored, sluggish, or apathetic.

REFERENCES

Bates, Marilyn. "A Test of Group Counseling," *Personnel and Guidance Journal,* April 1968, pp. 749-53.

Bessell, Harold. "The Content is the Medium: The Confidence is the Message," *Psychology Today,* Vol. 1, No. 8 (January 1968), p. 32.

_____ and Palomares, Uvaldo. *Methods in Human Development.* San Diego, CA: Human Development Training Institute, 1970.

Bigelow, Gordon S., and Thorne, John W. "Reality Versus Client-centered Models in Group Counseling," *School Counselor,* Vol. 16, No. 3 (January 1969), pp. 194-95.

Blaker, Kenneth E., and Bennett, Roger W. "Behavioral Counseling for Elementary School Children," *Elementary School Journal,* Vol. 70 (1970), pp. 411-17.

Canfield, Jack, and Wells, Harold C. *100 Ways to Enhance Self-concept in the Classroom.* Englewood Cliffs, NJ: Prentice-Hall, 1976.

Chase, Larry. *The Other Side of the Report Card.* Pacific Palisades, CA: Goodyear Publishing Co., 1975.

Dinkmeyer, Don C. *Developing Understanding in Self and Others.* DUSO D-2 *Kit.* Circle Pines, MN: American Guidance Service, 1973.

Gelatt, H.B., Varenhorst, Barbara, Carey, Richard, and Miller, Gordon P. *Decisions and Outcomes.* Princeton, NJ: College Entrance Examination Board, 1973.

Gibbs, Jeanne, and Allen, Andre. *TRIBES: A Human Development Process for Educational Systems.* Oakland, CA: Center Source Publications, 1978.

Hawley, Robert C., and Hawley, Isabel L. *A Handbook of Personal Growth Activities for Classroom Use.* Amherst, MA: Education Research Associates, 1972.

Hill, William F. "The Hill Interaction Matrix,"*Personnel and Guidance Journal,* Vol. 49, No. 8 (April 1971), pp. 619-22.

Johnson, Kenneth G., Senatore, John J., Liebig, Mark C., and Minor, Gene. *Nothing Never Happens.* Beverly Hills, CA: Glencoe Press, 1974.

King, Charles. "Activity Group Therapy," Mimeographed Paper, Los Angeles County Superintendent of Schools, Division of Research and Pupil Personnel Services, #37511, January 1967.

Limbacher, Walter J. *Becoming Myself.* Dayton, OH: Pflaum/Standard Publishers, 1969.

―――. *Here I am.* Dayton, OH: Pflaum/Standard Publishers, 1969.

―――. *I Am Not Alone.* Dayton, OH: Pflaum/Standard Publishers, 1970.

Los Angeles Unified School District. "A Guide to Group Counseling in Elementary Schools." Los Angeles: Division of Elementary Education, Guidance and Counseling Section, October, 1969 (revised).

Mayer, C. Roy, Rohen, Terrance, and Whitley, A. Dan. "Group Counseling With Children," *Journal of Counseling Psychology,* Vol. 16, No. 2 (1969), pp. 124-49.

Muro, James J., and Dinkmeyer, Don C. *Counseling in the Elementary and Middle Schools.* Dubuque, IA: Wm. C. Brown, 1977.

Otto, Herbert A. "Developing Student Potential," *California Elementary Administrator,* Vol. 33, No. 4 (May 1970), pp. 7-9.

―――. *A Guide To Developing Your Potential.* North Hollywood, CA: Wilshire Book Co., 1970.

Redl, F. "The Concept of the Life Space Interview," *American Journal of Orthopsychiatry,* Vol. 29 (1959), pp. 1-18.

_____. *When We Deal With Children*. New York: Free Press, 1966.

Reichert, Richard. *Self Awareness Through Group Dynamics*. Dayton, OH: Pflaum/Standard Publishers, 1970.

Simon, Sidney B., Howe, Leland W., and Kirschenbaum, Howard. *Values Clarification: A Handbook of Practical Strategies for Teachers and Students*. New York: Hart Publishing Co., 1972.

Tillinghast, B.S., Jr. "Needed: A Psychology of Joy For Children," *Guidepost*, Vol. 12, No. 9 (June 1970), p. 3.

10

The Extensional Group Model
in Community and Medical Settings

10

The Extensional Group Model
in Community and Medical Settings

In our opinion, group work has received "bad press," particularly during the late 1960s and early 1970s, when the "far-out," anti-establishment movement was attracting so much negative attention. Groups often became the forum in which values and culture issues were discussed, and group experiences were regarded suspiciously by conservative segments of our society as having some strange, insidious, *causal* potential. Although groups were definitely in vogue in the counter-culture movement, group work did not cause the upheavals in values and life-styles. During the time when an unpopular war, civil rights marches, assassinations, and moon walks monopolized our attention, we were in a period of incredibly rapid societal and value changes, and much confusion resulted. Group work was often maligned and misinterpreted as contributing to the social unrest. Thus, some conservatives were suspicious of, if not openly hostile to, group work.

It is true, however, that in a large segment of our society, groups had acquired a fadish mystique that attracted incompetent leaders and participants who were looking for miraculous psychological cures and instant intimacy and personal growth (Shostrom, 1970). A "groupie" cult began to emerge which not only distracted from spontaneous group interaction (because members began to *act* like they thought good group members *should)*, but also fostered the antithesis of independence and self-responsibility that group work is supposed to promote.

One of the authors recalls a conversation with an associate who frequently attended weekend encounter groups. The associate was expressing negative feelings about a third party (not present). When it was suggested that being "up front" with the other man might clear up the hard feelings, the associate replied, "That's a good idea. I'll do that the next time we're in a group together."

Sleepless weekend marathons, nude encounter groups, group massages, and reports of promiscuous sex made titillating copy for media coverage a decade ago. Indeed, some crazy, irresponsible, and sometimes harmful things were going on in the name of group work and personal growth. Such irresponsibility fueled the suspicions of those who wished to disparage group work, and, in one case at least, any form of group work was automatically categorized as part of the Communists' efforts to brainwash and misguide the youth of our nation (Allen, 1968). Highly respected group researchers tried to sort out the good from the bad, the effective from the ineffective (Lieberman, Yalom, & Miles, 1973), only to be criticized (Schutz, 1974) by researchers of equally respected stature. During the late 1960s and early 1970s few people were neutral about group work. It was a period of vigorous debate on many issues, including the merits of group participation.

Becoming a participant in a new group still provokes sweaty palms and increased heart rate, even in extensional groups where human dignity and respect are paramount. The unknown element associated with getting to know others and allowing ourselves to be known to others is exciting. It starts the adrenalin flowing, and in some cases can be downright scary. These kinds of reactions, which also occur in nongroup situations, compounded the negative public attitudes toward group work. Fortunately, those negative attitudes are mellowing. The increasing numbers and varieties of group settings attest to the fact that groups do not create the intense reactions, pro or con, that they once did.

To illustrate the increasing acceptance of group work, this chapter gives an overview of various settings in which group participation is an important part. Presented generically as "groups in community and medical settings," the overview reflects the range of purposes and situations in which the extensional group model has been adapted. Not all of the groups described in the paragraphs that follow are aware of the term "extensional" or the concept it labels. The groups described below were selected because the format they use is consistent with the model promoted herein. Through this book, we are advocating a model that we think has tremendous potential for effectiveness and diversity. The extensional group model may or may not be effective as a therapeutic (remedial) strategy in some cases, but if focusing on strengths is a desired goal, the extensional group model is effective. By referring to Figure 1.1 on page 8, the reader will recall the area of overlap between the two concepts of group: extensional and remedial.

Cancer patients have intense concerns about health and therapy. This is understandable. The patients, however, are encouraged to examine their strengths and resources for improving their condition, not necessarily for curing it. A spiritual awakening at a religious retreat, for example, can carry with it the potential for confusion and guilt feelings, as well as the potential for euphoria. The extensional group model attempts to direct attention toward growth aspects of the experience. Euphoria without a realistic perspective is not good. Hopeless despair, with confusion and guilt, is likewise undesirable. Extensional group experiences have been beneficial in improving these human conditions. Mutual support, *without pressure* to change, serves a tremendously humanitarian purpose. That is the message we hope to convey in the following illustrations.

COMMUNITY SETTINGS

Senior Citizens Groups

Get Up and Go Group

The "Get Up and Go" group in San Jose, California, directed by Judy Ostrow, is conducted from an extensional group model. The group includes 14 to 16 participants who attend eight 1½-hour weekly sessions in the offices of the Independent Aging Program (a privately funded service agency for elderly who live at home). The advertising brochure describes the group as a forum in which common problems can be discussed and a place to meet new friends.

Because terms and phrases such as "psychology," "counseling," and "mental health," generally suffer from negative stereotypical biases among this age group, they are assiduously avoided. As one elderly lady put it, "I'd rather see a mortician than see a psychologist!" To many people of this age bracket, anyone who accepts mental health attention is admitting to being sick or crazy.

A great deal of life review, personal exploration, and mutual support occurs in the "Get Up and Go" group, and whether or not the process should be called "counseling" is irrelevant. The group provides beneficial service that would otherwise be unavailable to these elderly people. For example, one of the participants had recently been prohibited from driving his automobile because his medication made him unpredictably drowsy. In this gentleman's mind he had been deprived of the last vestige of his independence, and he was quite depressed. The group, which knew of his values and life-style from previous group sessions, gently but persistently reminded him of several areas of his life in which he was more independent and more fortunate than many other elderly people. He was financially secure in his retirement, lived in his own home, was within walking distance of friends and relatives, and still had good use of his faculties.

Creative Arts Group for the Elderly

Navarra and Blaker (in press) applied a variation of the extensional group model in which creative activities are used as catalytic exercises. Their project was inspired by work done at SAGE (Senior Actualization and Growth Exploration) in Berkeley, California (Powell & Pruess, 1978; Dychtwald, 1979), an organization devoted to revitalizing the minds, bodies, and spirits of the elderly. Interpersonal interaction plays a large part and activities are introduced according to the needs of the emerging group. Some of the activities are more structured than those previously described in this book. Guided imagery, creative dance, physical exercise, massage, and role-playing are sequenced activities. They are followed by discussions for the purpose of building confidence and self-esteem. The group attempts to capitalize on *intra-* as well as *inter*personal experience.

Lifespring

In 1974 a group of educators and businessmen developed Lifespring, a nonprofit organization dedicated to the human potential movement. Although Lifespring does not represent any single philosophy or psychological theory, it is strongly influenced by the teachings of Carl Rogers, Abraham Maslow, Fritz Perls, and Gordon Allport, all of whom have emphasized the importance of positive views of humankind as the foundation for self-directed growth. Lifespring's training sessions are relatively structured by time and include exercises and meditation. About 25 percent of the time is devoted to guided group interaction similar to that of the extensional group process. Members are encouraged, but not pressed, to reveal their here-and-now experiences that are stimulated from the exercises and meditations. Businessmen, clergy, teachers, couples, *anyone* who believes in the human's potential for positive change may wish to consider Lifespring as a personal and/or professional resource. Lifespring, with headquarters in San Rafael, California, has offices throughout the United States and Canada.

Church Groups

Sharing Groups

Leslie's book (1971) about using group process in church work is highly practical (especially Chapters 7 and 8) and was a daring publication at the time. Spiritual development has normally been thought of as an *intra*personal process, usually influenced, but not necessarily shared with, a knowledgeable outside person (rabbi, minister, priest, retreat director, etc.). The intrapersonal nature of spiritual development remains a primary growth experience, but a new dimension is being introduced as formal religion struggles for current ways to help keep the faith and spread the gospel. Leslie's notion of congregational involvement via group work includes spiritual exploration, personal growth considerations, religious education, and church governance. The small group is not a basic format for exercising religious faith, but it is becoming an important adjunct that has only recently been seriously considered. Married couples, singles groups, women's groups, and youth groups are included in Leslie's concept of congregational involvement, and he sees it as an effective means for creating a true sense of community within the church.

Jesuit Institute for Family Life

Traditionally ministers, rabbis, priests, and other religious workers have spent a major part of their energies and efforts serving their congregations in the form of spiritual and personal counseling. Pastoral counseling is commonly founded on faith, love, and optimism — beautiful and important qualities, but insufficient for assuring effective counseling. In California in the 1960s, a Marriage, Family, and Child Counseling license was issued to any ordained minister who applied, regardless of the presence or lack of training and expertise in counseling psychology. As pastoral training and sophistication improve, and as social problems intensify, religious workers look for professional counseling assistance that is consistent with religious beliefs.

The Jesuit Institute for Family Life, Los Altos, California, was created in 1977 and is staffed with highly qualified medical and psychological professionals, most of whom are members of religious orders within the Catholic church. It is directed by Fr.

Robert Fabing. The staff offers consulting services to parish priests and counseling for couples and families who wish to enrich existing positive relationships or to rectify relational disruptions. Group work, using the equivalent of the extensional group model, is a significant part of the services provided.

Wilson House for Adolescents

In Santa Clara, California, a publicly funded program, the Bill Wilson House (sometimes referred to as the "Runaway House") was developed for counseling adolescents who wish to have a respite from troubled family situations. The problem may be entirely domestic or it might be complicated by the adolescents' illegal activities. Since the program includes temporary residential care, milieu therapy is a vital part of Wilson House (under the directorship of Jackie Martin). Milieu therapy, as applied at Wilson House, encourages openness and self-disclosure among the staff and residents, for purposes of strength building. The program insists that the adolescent's family be a part of the strength building process. In addition to conducting groups for staff and residents, Wilson House provides support groups for parents who are concerned about their adolescent children. Although the extensional group model is not consciously implemented at Wilson House, the process of self-disclosure, feedback, interaction, and mutual support is completely within the model described in previous chapters of this book.

MEDICAL SETTINGS

Holistic medicine is an emerging concept that promotes the power of mutual caring and support as a therapeutic strategy for health problems, even severe and terminal health problems, such as some cancers. Although the term "therapy" is used in these group contexts, it does not completely fit the remedial character of therapy groups described in the first chapter. In the

247

groups described below the special attention to personal strength and emotional resources characterizes a collective process consistent with the extensional group model.

Groups for Children Who Are Ill

Gerald G. Jampolsky (1979a, 1979b), a psychiatrist in Tiburon, California, has specialized in treating children who are victims of catastrophic illnesses, and one of his principal treatment modalities has been group participation of children with similar afflictions. Jampolsky focuses on love, positive thinking, and reciprocal support. Most of his patients are seriously ill, and the possibility of cure, in the strictest sense of therapy, is remote. Quality of living while life exists is more the issue in his groups than is the hope for a remission of the illness. The collective strength shown by Jampolsky's young patients is remarkable and moving, and probably would go unheeded if not for Jampolsky's sensitive and perceptive approach to capitalizing on the available strengths of ill young people.

El Camino Hospital's Department of Human Support

Dan Dugan has modified the extensional group model to supplement the training and experience of his staff (professional and volunteer) and students. The primary work of the Department of Human Support is to aid patients and families of patients who are seriously, and often terminally, ill in coping with the mental and emotional stress that naturally accompanies health problems. Professional caregivers in this setting need their own sources of sustenance and stress reduction. Twelve two-hour weekly sessions are offered to groups of 15-20 participants who are being trained in stress reduction and emotional support services. Hospital staff members are encouraged to attend these training sessions, and patients, family members, and physicians are invited as guest participants. Catalytic activities in the form of films, discussions, readings, and experiential exercises are used in a manner similar to the

248

extensional group process. The activities allow for considerable spontaneous interaction.

Groups for Institutionalized Elderly

Burnside's (1978) seminal group work with the elderly in convalescent hospitals provided guidance for using the extensional group model with alert convalescing patients. "Alert" elderly are distinguished from the less alert by the degree to which they have control of their faculties. Patients who are sedated or whose severity of organic brain dysfunctioning qualifies them for a reality orientation or remotivation group do not do well in an extensional type of group. Their short attention span, absence of interpersonal interest, and lack of perspective detract from more alert members' participation. Mentally alert elders, in contrast, possess all their normal interests and concerns; many of them are confined to a convalescent facility because they cannot care for themselves at home (e.g., recovering from a broken hip).

A major psychological problem for patients in convalescent hospitals is the isolation and loneliness they frequently experience. Roommates may not know each other's names or anything about each other, although they intimately share the same living space. For patients with a reasonable degree of alertness, group work of an extensional nature is helpful in relieving some of the loneliness.

When working with groups of institutionalized elderly, some unique problems should be considered. The extensional group model emphasizes the importance of interaction in the here and now. For convalescing elderly the here and now may not be too pleasant, and it is easier for them to reminisce about the past or to complain. Complaint themes are common when working with groups like these ("My orderly would do such and such." "My doctor is not being completely truthful with me." "No one around here cares"). Group leaders must exert special efforts to keep the interaction among convalescing elderly positive and in the present. One such positive environment is created by Scott Heffner at the Pleasant View Convalescent Hospital in Cupertino, California.

249

SUMMARY

Group work has survived adulation and derision. "Group-ies" extolled the benefits they thought they would gain by participating in groups, and the conservatives condemned what they thought was subversive. Having survived the tests of the extremes, group work is maturing and is finally achieving the recognition and sensible attention it deserves. Helping people learn how to help themselves improve their lives is a noble effort, and group work is *one* sensible and practical way of doing that. The range and purposes of group work described in Chapter 10 attest to the value of group work in various settings and among people with widely variant circumstances and needs.

REFERENCES

Allen, Gary. "Hate Therapy — Sensitivity Training for Planned Change," *American Opinion*, January 1968.

Burnside, Irene Mortenson. *Working with the Elderly: Group Processes and Techniques*. Belmont, CA: Duxbury Press, 1978.

Dychtwald, Ken. "Aging: The Elder Within," *New Age*, February 1979, pp. 29-33.

Jampolsky, G., and Taylor, P. "Peer and Self Healing in Children" in E. Goldwag (Ed.), *Inner Balance: The Power of Holistic Healing*. Englewood Cliffs, NJ: Prentice-Hall, 1979. (a)

Jampolsky, G. *Love is Letting Go of Fear*. Millbrae, CA: Celestial Arts, 1979. (b)

Leslie, Robert C. *Sharing Groups in Church: An Invitation to Involvement*. Nashville, TN; Abingdon Press, 1971.

Lieberman, Morton A., Yalom, Irvin D., and Miles, Matthew B. *Encounter Groups: First Facts*. New York: Basic Books, 1973.

Navarra, Robert, and Blaker, Kenneth E. "Creative Group Work with the Elderly," *Personnel & Guidance Journal*, in press.

Powell, Carol, and Pruess, Karen. "SAGE: Reshaping Attitudes About Aging," *Second Spring*, August/September 1978, pp. 3-7.

Schutz, William C. "Not Encounter and Certainly Not Facts," a review of *Encounter Groups: First Facts* by Morton Lieberman, Irvin Yalom, and Matthew Miles in the 1974 *Annual Handbook for Group Facilitators*, J. William Pfeiffer and John E. Jones, eds. San Diego, CA: University Associates, Inc. 1974.

Shostrom, Everett L. "Group Therapy: Let The Buyer Beware" in *Readings in Psychology Today*. Del Mar, CA: CRM Books, 1970, pp. 149-51.

APPENDIX A

Historical Foundations

The cognitive gestalt by which group leaders guide their behavior throughout the group process may not always be in their awareness. They may not be able to explicate a theoretical model of either group process or of human personality, but they are making decisions continuously based on at least some implicit assumptions concerning both the process and human nature. Professional pride as well as professional competency would suggest that an understanding of the implications of various models is the basis from which group leaders should work out their own theoretical foundation.

The following comments identify four common models, define the cognitive map of humanity underlying each model, suggest the parameters of the leader's role, and specify resultant techniques. The functions of group members are identified, followed by goals derived from the basic model. A final comment relates to various extensions of the model as practiced currently. An outline at the end of the appendix summarizes this discussion for the reader's convenience.

PSYCHOANALYTICAL MODEL

Cognitive Map

The cognitive map whereby group leaders working from a psychoanalytical frame of reference govern their behavior is, of course, Freud's id-ego-superego. Elaborating on this well-known construct is not contemplated here. Rather, attention will be given to its applications to the group process.

Group Model

In the psychoanalytical model the group represents the early family constellation. Thus, significant experiences that occurred in each group member's own family, including early childhood events, are to be "worked through," and it is hoped that as a result, insight will emerge. The assumption is made that if the dynamics of unresolved conflicts are understood, negative effects of the conflict will be removed. It is expected that during group interaction each member will project onto other members his or her own needs, perceptions, distortions, defenses, and so forth, which arise from past and present interactions with significant others outside the group. The material produced concerning these conflicts, interactions, and perceptions are to be analyzed by the group. It is expected that the group members will learn more ego-controlled behaviors and be less governed by id-controlled behavior. Learning is assumed to be toward the rational and away from the irrational.

Leader's Role

In the psychoanalytical model leaders serve as symbolic authority figures. They may at times represent father, mother, teacher, or all three simultaneously. They also serve as a symbolic superego against which group members test their own superego precepts. The leader who works within the psycho-analytical framework helps members recall "forgotten" childhood memories, attempts to aid members to reality-test and to understand dynamics of their own and others' behaviors, eventually verbalizing insights.

Techniques

Techniques derived from the psychoanalytical model include procedures appropriate in individual therapy, such as dream analysis, free association, and recall of early childhood

254

memories. The leader encourages transference, while being alert to counter-transference. He or she and group members analyze and interpret projective behaviors and defense mechanisms. Verbal behavior of the leader and members includes probing, analyzing, questioning, interpreting, and supporting.

Functions of Group Members

In the psychoanalytical model the group leader expects members to function as assistant therapists. Members also function in the roles of each member's early family constellation — siblings, parents, etc. Therefore, the content of the group often includes quarrels, hostilities, and regressive behavior as the members "act out" earlier conflicts.

Group Members' Goals

Members' goals in the psychoanalytical model of the group process are individualized by the therapist according to each member's needs but may include desensitization of painful and traumatic past experiences, may clarify for members their "authority" problems, may lessen a member's need to protect his or her id impulses through use of excessive ego defense mechanisms, may free spontaneity, especially in the area of sexual expression, and may help group members handle identity crises.

Extensions of the Model

One extension of the psychoanalytical model is represented by the marathon format, which makes the assumption that under the pressure of continuous group interaction, aided by loss of sleep, the ego defenses of group members are lowered and the core of personality is more available for analysis and insight.

255

Berne's (1961) *Transactional Analysis* extends the ego of the Freudian construct into three ego states: parent, child, and adult. The transactions conducted from each of these three ego states are analyzed in the group process. Various "games" people "play" in their interactions with each other are identified. This represents much of the content of group work. The life script of each member is clarified so that behavior can be controlled increasingly by the adult ego state.

PHENOMENOLOGICAL MODEL

Cognitive Map

In the phenomenological model the cognitive map the group leader uses describes humans as seeking, striving organisms with an innate drive toward psychological health. Group members each contain their own "truth" as it is perceived in their idiosyncratic world. The group leader attempts to understand and to enter the phenomenological world of each member and tries to be alert to discrepancies between a member's internalized ideal self and his or her perceived real self, for this discrepancy is seen as the cause of maladjustment. Psychological health requires harmony between the real and the ideal self.

Group Model

The group environment is designed to create a threat-free oasis where members can examine their self-concepts. The focus of group content is on each individual's perceptions of his or her world rather than on the relationships between members, per se. Since self-concepts are seen as based primarily in the affective domain, the emphasis of the interaction is on *feelings* rather than on ideas.

Leader's Role

Leaders in the phenomenological group attempt to create and maintain a threat-free, permissive atmosphere through their own expressions of acceptance, unconditional regard, and respect. They help members enter each other's phenomenological world, and they attempt to make members aware of their self-concepts by responding to *feelings,* both overt and covert, and by encouraging congruency between feelings and behavior. The leader provides a model of congruency.

Techniques

To label behaviors that follow from the phenomenological model "techniques" is a misnomer, for the group leaders mainly exhibit an *attitude* of caring, accepting, and understanding. They understand the idiosyncratic worlds of members. They gain this understanding through intensive, skilled listening, and their chief speech patterns are reflections of feelings, clarification of feelings and ideas, acceptance statements, and unstructured general leads. They perform a linking function as they attempt to help members perceive contradictions between their ideal and their real selves. They consistently respond to conative (affective) content rather than to cognitive content. The group situation is left unstructured deliberately so as to create an ambiguous situation in which group members can explore their own phenomenological fields. Leaders may use techniques of immediate feedback via videotape to help members meet their "real" selves. Leaders also may use sensory experiences to increase members' awareness of ongoing visceral processes and emotional reactions.

Functions of Group Members

Members of the phenomenological group serve as mirrors in which group participants can check perceptions, distortions,

257

values, and so on. Members are encouraged to "care" for other members so that the natural growth forces toward goodness can be released. Members provide "human nourishment" for one another.

Group Members' Goals

The primary goal of the nondirective phenomenological group is the maximum self-actualization of each member. This is achieved by bringing conative processes into awareness so that members are each able to experience another dimension of living. The innate drive toward the good is released in each member.

Extensions of the Model

Early basic encounter groups were based on the phenomenological model, and current "sensitivity" groups seem based on similar assumptions concerning human nature. The Western Behavioral Science Institute's Encountertapes (tape-recorder-led groups) published by Bell and Howell assume that leaderless groups are satisfactory, and thus must make the assumption of the phenomenologists that we are by nature "good."

BEHAVIORAL MODEL

Cognitive Map

The behavioral model conceptualizes humans as reactive organisms: Stimulus, bond, Response. The emphasis is on the "S" and the "R," and these are observable. People can be shaped to conform to desired behavior through reinforcement techniques.

Group Model

Under the group leader's direction, the group process can be used to reinforce desired behaviors. The group is the social microcosm that represents the societal macrocosm, and the assumption is made that learning appropriate behavior in the former will generalize to the latter. Roles must be learned, and the group is seen as providing a learning situation in which new ways of behaving can be experienced.

Leader's Role

The role of the leader in the behavioral model is to shape members' behaviors.

Techniques

Use of reinforcement is consistent in the behavioral model. Group leaders attend selectively — using both verbal and nonverbal feedback to respond to behaviors they perceive as desirable. "Role modeling" through audio tape is used to provide an example of appropriate behavior. The verbalization of the leader includes approval, disapproval, and leading questions; it stresses operational specificity and cognitive content. Group leaders use their own behavior as a reinforcement model. They also serve as a source of factual information and a source of value judgments.

Functions of Group Members

Group members reinforce desired behavior in others under the group leader's guidance.

259

Group Members' Goals

In the behavioral model group goals are in terms of enculturation rather than individuation — i.e., adjustment to the school setting, increased vocational exploration, educational adjustment, and so forth. Objectives, however, are to be highly specific for each member and couched in operational terms. The emphasis is on observable behavior both in and out of the group.

Extensions of the Model

John Krumboltz's (1964) "Behavioral Counseling Groups" are based on a behavioral model. Leaders and members together specify desired behaviors. The leader reinforces these behaviors and primarily attempts to enculturate.

EXISTENTIAL MODEL

Cognitive Map

The existential model is based on a philosophical rather than a psychological view of humanity. People are seen as existing with no "givens," and their task in life is to define themselves through their creations (actions). As they experience "existential moments," they become more and more aware of themselves. These events — existential moments — begin in early adolescence, and from that time on people are responsible totally for all their actions. Henceforth, they are condemned to freedom to choose both for themselves and for all people. Because of this profound freedom, each of us suffers a human loneliness and anguish. We can assuage our loneliness through the encounter as we relate to one another I-to-Thou.

260

Group Members' Goals

Group members' goals of the existential model are to clarify self-definitions, to extend potentials, and to extend abilities to sustain intimacy (i.e., encounters). The group functions to alleviate our essential loneliness through emphatic feedback. The group helps members attain authenticity more consistently, and each member strives toward self-actualization. Members experience increased awareness of their essential state of freedom and become more and more aware of the attendant responsibility. The group attempts to help each member increase the choices he or she makes in awareness.

Extensions of the Model

Carl Rogers' current Basic Encounter Groups (Hart & Tomlinson, 1970) seem to be derived from an existential frame of reference. Glasser (1966) emphasized the concepts of responsibility and reality-testing that are consonant with existentialist philosophy. Gestalt (Fagan & Shepherd, 1970; Perls, 1970) approaches, which focus on the here and now, are consistent with the existentialist approach to group processes.

ECLECTIC MODEL

In the final analysis each group leader must formulate his or her own unique model. Thus, in a sense each leader is eclectic. The eclecticism, however, must stem from a thorough grounding in theoretical formulation, not from inadequate intellectual preparation. Effective leaders develop their own leadership style — the one most consonant with their strengths and limitations.

Group Model

The group exists in the only relevance — the here and the now — and exists for the only relevancy — the I-Thou relationship. Group members each make their statement about themselves through interfacing with others as authentically as possible. The uniqueness of the group process lies in the opportunity it provides for multiple feedback and for multiple encounters. Confrontation is seen as the most productive level of interaction.

Leader's Role

The role of leaders in the existential model is I-to-Thou in interaction. They risk themselves through their authentic relating to group members. They attempt to focus content on the "here and now" rather than on the "there and then." They interact on a personal level, are open and known rather than anonymous and knowing. In their verbal behavior they return consistently to the existent moment, reflect both feelings and ideas, link, clarify, make risk-taking statements that center risk in self, and constantly share themselves with group members.

Techniques

Existentialist group leaders make frequent use of confrontation, but do not attack. They attempt to help members clarify alternatives that pave the way for action choices outside the group. These action possibilities are specific. They use interaction techniques to generate immediate productive experiences for group members. The leader's self is the main technique that is ethically available to the counselor. This risk-taking centers on self.

OUTLINE

PSYCHOANALYTICAL MODEL

Cognitive Map: Id, ego, superego.

Group Model:
1. Group represents family.
2. Significant experiences worked through.
3. Basic assumption: If dynamics of unresolved conflicts are understood, negative cathexis of conflict is removed.
4. Members project onto other members interactions with significant others outside the group.
5. Materials from projections are analyzed; behavior becomes more ego-controlled than id-controlled, or rational rather than irrational.

Leader's Role:
1. To serve as symbolic authority figure.
2. To serve as symbolic superego.
3. To help members recall "forgotten" childhood memories.
4. To aid insight through verbalization.

Techniques:
1. Dream analysis.
2. Encourage transference; be alert to counter-transference.
3. Free association.
4. Analyze and interpret projective behavior.
5. Analyze and interpret defense mechanisms.
6. Verbal behavior: probing, analyzing, questioning, interpreting, supporting.

Functions of Group Members:
1. Serve as assistant therapists.
2. Serve in roles of each member's early family constellation — siblings, parents, etc.

Group Members' Goals:
1. To desensitize painful/traumatic past experiences.
2. To clarify "authority" hangups.
3. To lessen members' needs to protect id through ego defense mechanisms.
4. To free spontaneity, especially in sexual expression.
5. To help group members handle identify crises.

Extensions of Model:
1. Bach (1967): Marathon format.
2. Berne (1966): Transactional Analysis.
3. Moreno (1945): Psychodrama, Sociodrama (Spectator theory).

PHENOMENOLOGICAL MODEL

Cognitive Map:
1. Seeking, striving organism with innate drive toward mental health.
2. Imbalance because of discrepancy between ideal and real selves.
3. Truth is perceived idiosyncratically.

Group Model:
1. Threat-free environment in which members examine self-concepts.
2. Focus on individual's perception of world.
3. Emphasis on affect rather than cognition.

Leader's Role:
1. Create and maintain a threat-free, permissive atmosphere through own behavior.
2. Help members enter each other's phenomenological world.
3. Make members aware of their self-concepts by responding to *feelings* (overt and covert) and encouraging congruency between feelings and behavior.

Techniques:
1. Verbalize feelings, responding to conative content.
2. Transmit caring through verbalizing understanding that is gained through intensive, skilled listening.
3. Verbal behavior: reflection, clarification, linking, acceptance statements, general leads. Avoid structuring comments.
4. Deliberately create ambiguous, unstructured group environment so group members can create own phenomenological fields.
5. Use "focused feedback" through videotape to help members meet selves.
6. Use sensory experience to increase awareness of visceral processes.

Functions of Group Members:
1. Serve as mirrors in which group members can check their perceptions, distortions, values, etc.
2. Transmit "caring" of other members so that natural growth forces toward "goodness" can be released. Members provide "human nourishment" to each other.

Group Members' Goals:
1. Maximum self-actualization of each member.
2. Bring conative processes into awareness.

BEHAVIORAL MODEL

Cognitive Map:
Stimulus, bond, Response, with emphasis on "S" and "R."

Group Model:
1. Laboratory setting used to reinforce desired behaviors under leader's direction.
2. Social microcosm representing societal macrocosm.

Leader's Role:
Shape members' behaviors.

Techniques:
1. Reinforce desired behavior through attending selectively using verbal and nonverbal feedback as reinforcers.
2. Role modeling through audiotape (Krumboltz & Thoresen, 1964).
3. Verbal behavior: approval, disapproval, leading questions, emphasizing cognitive content, emphasizing operational specificity.
4. Use systems analysis approach to problem solving.
5. Use own behavior as reinforcement model.
6. Provide information.

Functions of Group Members:
To reinforce other members' behaviors under group leader's guidance.

Group Members' Goals:
1. Very specific for each member.
2. Specified in operational terms by group leader before group begins.
3. Emphasis on *observable* behavior in and out of group.

Extension of Model:
Krumboltz's (1964) "Vocational Guidance Groups."

EXISTENTIAL MODEL

Cognitive Map:
1. We exist with no "givens"; must define self.
2. We are condemned to freedom to choose for ourselves and all people.

Group Model:
1. Group exists in the "here and now."
2. Group exists for I-Thou relationship.
3. Members make statements about selves through interfacing as authentically as possible.
4. Group is unique in feedback and encounter.

Leader's Role:
1. To open self I-to-Thou as model.
2. Risk self through sharing self in creating encounters.
3. Through verbalizations, to keep focus on here and now rather than on there and then.
4. Through verbalization, to keep focus on I-to-Thou rather than he/she and it.
5. Verbal behavior: Return constantly to existing moment, reflect feelings and ideas, link, clarify, make risk-taking statements, center risk on self.

Techniques:
1. Make frequent use of confrontation, avoiding attack.
2. Clarify alternatives to pave way for action choices.
3. Specify action possibilities.
4. Self is main instrument ethically available to counselor.

Functions of Group Members:
1. To relate to each other on I-to-Thou basis.
2. To extend life spaces of members.
3. To provide human nourishment.

Group Members' Goals:
1. To clarify self-definitions of members.
2. To extend abilities of members to sustain intimacy (encounters).
3. To alleviate members' essential loneliness through empathic feedback.
4. To assist members in reaching authentic behavior more frequently.

5. Self-actualization of each member.
6. To make each member more aware of his or her essential state of freedom with its attendant responsibility.
7. To help members increase numbers of choices they make in awareness.

Extensions of Model:
1. Rogers' (1970) current Basic Encounter Groups.
2. Gestalt (Perls, 1970).
3. Extensional model (Bates & Johnson, 1970).

ECLECTIC MODEL

Cognitive Map: ?
Group Model: ?
Leader's Role: ?
Techniques: Any and all of above.
Functions of Members: ?
Group Members' Goals: ?
Extensions of Model: Almost any group?

BIBLIOGRAPHY

Bach, George R. "Marathon Group Dynamics: I. Some Functions of the Professional Group Facilitator," *Psychological Reports*, Vol. 20 (July 1967), pp. 995-999.

Berne, Eric. *Principles of Group Treatment.* New York: Oxford University Press, 1966.

Bradford, Leland; Gibb, Jack; and Benne, Kenneth. *T-Group Theory and Laboratory Method: Innovation in Re-education.* New York: Wiley and Sons, 1964.

Encounter Tapes, Leader-less Group Tapes, Western Behavioral Science Institute, La Jolla, CA.

Fagan, Joen, and Shepherd, Irma Lee. *Gestalt Therapy Now.* Palo Alto, CA: Science and Behavior Books, 1970.

Glasser, William, and Iverson, Norman. *Large Group Counseling.* Los Angeles: Reality Press, 1966.

Hart, J. T., and Tomlinson, T. M. *New Directions in Client-Centered Therapy*. Boston: Houghton Mifflin, 1970.

Krumboltz, John, and Thoresen, Carl. "The Effect of Behavioral Counseling in Group and Individual Settings on Information-Seeking Behavior," *Journal of Counseling Psychology*, Vol. II, 1964, pp. 324-335.

Moreno, J. L., Ed. *Group Psychotherapy*. Beacon, NY: Beacon Press, 1945.

Otto, Herbert, Ed. *Explorations in Human Potentialities*. Springfield, IL: Charles C Thomas, 1966.

Perls, Frederick S. *Gestalt Therapy Verbatim*. Palo Alto, CA: Science and Behavior Books, 1970.

Rogers, Carl R. "The Process of the Basic Encounter Group," in *New Directions in Client-Centered Therapy*, edited by Hart and Tomlinson. Boston: Houghton Mifflin, 1970.

APPENDIX B

Open Letter:
An Induction Tool for Adults

To: A Fellow Group Member
From: A Co-member
Re: Open Letter

Dear _____:

I just found out that we are going to be in group together and am
delighted that I will have the opportunity to interact with you. Since
we will be traveling unknown territory, I would like to share with you
some of the thoughts I have concerning this experience. If you are like
me, you are not quite sure of the rules. Something is expected of us,
and I most certainly expect to get something out of it or I wouldn't
have joined. Just *what* is rather unclear at this point. You most likely
share some of the anxieties I am experiencing and might be interested
in my thoughts as I approach this new, rather frightening experience.

First of all, I am wondering what it's going to be like — this being
called "group." I've heard some bad things about groups — tales of
people being stripped of their defenses and left there, tales of super-
emotional binges that left people wondering what happened the next
day, descriptions of personal privacy being probed in a way that
amounted to psychological voyeurism. You, as I, have heard of groups
in which members and leaders seemed to gain what amounted to
masochistic-sadistic "kicks" watching individual members being torn
to shreds in the name of the "new honesty" and "gut-level sensitivity."
I would not care to experience all these things, and as protection I

carefully selected a leader who, because of his [her] competency and theoretical orientation, had control of the group process and could block destructive elements.

I believe that group *can* be a very good thing — exciting, stimulating, joyous, and growth-motivating. I expect to gain some specific things from the interaction. For one thing, I hope that I will become less defensive and learn to know and express my feelings more accurately. I also hope I can release more self-actualizing forces within me and maybe even give up manipulative behaviors altogether. I most certainly want to increase my ability to establish and maintain tax-free relationships. I hope I will learn to express more freely a caring for others and perhaps even come to care more for *me*. I do look forward to being able to experience encounters more frequently, and maybe I will even be able to develop the intuitiveness I have observed in others who have been in groups for sensing open, nondefensive people. I would wish that my sense of alienation would diminish and that my spontaneity in responding to others would increase. I hope my hunger for resonance will be met, as you and others in our group share how it is with you with me. In simple terms, I guess I see group as a source of human nourishment to me.

I am aware that I cannot depend only on the group leader or other members to make the group experience a positive one. I am keenly conscious of the responsibilities I carry now that I have committed myself to group membership. First of all, I see myself as contracting with all of you to participate in the interaction. Inevitably I will *react*, but I know that I must also *interact*. Just as I hope to obtain resonance from you, I will expect to provide you with feedback on how I am experiencing you. I know I am the only one who can tell you how it is with me — how I am reacting to you. If I withhold this information from you, I am not meeting my obligations to you as a fellow group member. I will probably want to hide behind silence at times, and I know it will take courage on my part to take the risk of telling you how I am reacting to you. You may reject me whether my reactions are positive or negative, and this thought makes me anxious. I am quite conscious of my inadequacies in accurately transmitting my emotions and thoughts, and I hope you will be patient with me as I struggle to communicate. I also hope you and all the group members will remember that I never really am talking about you, no matter what I say, but always about me. In turn, I know the reverse is true — that, as you react to me, you really are making statements about you — never about me. If I choose to internalize your observations because they seem useful and accurate, I can do so, but I do not want to experience being judged by you or to experience judging you. This would diminish both of us, whether we are judge or judger.

As a group member, I perceive that I have entered into other obligations. For example, I agree that what occurs in our group remains there. I do not expect to transmit to another, no matter how close he or she is, what happens in our group. This belongs to us and only to us. I also realize that I have an obligation to attend all meetings if I possibly can. I am aware that my absence sends a message that I had a choice to make and that my priority was not our group.

As I experience group with you, I hope I do not intrude into your private life space. I also reserve on my part the right to introduce into the group only the things I choose from my life outside the group. As we interact, there will be so much going on "here and now" that most of our "there and then" experiences would be an intrusion. I would rather that we expended our time and energies on responding to each other, really listening and hearing *meanings,* not just words. I also will try to be sensitive to your nonverbal communications, to respond to your body language and your voice intonations, as well as your spoken words. I hope I can be open and authentic and share my feelings, thoughts, and experiencings with you, rather than relate to you as an object. I want you to experience me as there and available — a subject to be communicated with, not an object to be dissected.

I do not expect that our journey together will always be comfortable. As we encounter each other, we may have moments of confrontation that involve hostility, but I hope I don't deny to you expression of those feelings, nor you to me, though neither of us may be pleased with them. I want you to accept and understand my conflicts, just as I hope I can accept and understand yours. I would hope that you really try to help me solve problems I may choose to bring to the group, and that I can do the same for you. If, however, you find me giving advice or interceding in your efforts to face a situation fully, I hope you will point this out. I'm sure that as you provide feedback to me — I-to-Thou — I will come to understand myself better and will gain in knowledge of myself. I will try to express honest warmth and acceptance if I feel this way, and I hope that if you feel these things, you will express them to me. I hope the group will become empathic as we share ourselves. If I experience too much coldness, or noncaring, or indifference, I think I will leave. Those responses would diminish me, and I do not choose to be diminished by the group process. I do choose to try to communicate as fully as possible, to give and receive

273

confrontation, and to give and receive encounters. I am certain that there *is* life after birth, and I believe that group is one way to find it. I would like to try.

Sincerely,

APPENDIX C

So You Are Going To Be in Group Counseling: An Induction Tool for Students

To the Student:

This pamphlet was written to help answer some of your questions about group counseling. You will find included some questions that have been asked by other students concerning group counseling which may be helpful in explaining how you will fit in group counseling. You may have other questions or thoughts to discuss so please feel free to ask your counselor.

What Is Group Counseling?

Group counseling can mean many things to many people, but it provides an opportunity to:
1. talk about common concerns or problems
2. express your feelings in a small group
3. help you to understand how you are seen by others.

How Often Do We Meet?

The group will meet at least one period a week for a number of weeks that your counselor has suggested. Meetings will begin on time and end on time.

Who Is Going To Be in the Group?

We will have at least one counselor and 5 to 10 other students who have expressed an interest in discussing their feelings, goals, and other interests. The group members may

275

be all girls, all boys, or sometimes both. Very seldom are more than two grade levels represented.

What Can I Gain by Being in a Group?

1. You may come to understand others in the group more clearly.
2. This understanding of others can help you to see and evaluate yourself more clearly.
3. You may gain an understanding of your strengths and benefit from these.
4. It gives you a place to express yourself and your feelings.
5. You may find you have concerns similar to others in the group and realize that you are not alone.

What Will Be Expected of Me?

Some of the things the group would expect of you would be:
1. to be there on time
2. to be honest
3. be willing to listen to the others
4. be willing to respond to others.

Do I Have To Be in the Group?

No, but we would like you to be if you want to.

Can I Quit the Group?

You may leave the group any time you wish to do so.

Would You Like to Reserve a Place? ⸺⸺⸺

Your Objectives:

Thanks is given to Al Finlayson, Counselor, Orange Unified School District, Orange, California, for his permission to use this pamphlet.

Index

280

I wish to acknowledge my debt of gratitude to Fr. Leo Rock, S. J., who introduced me to group work almost two decades ago, and also to Terry Dyckman, who educated me as to the practical applications of group theory and technique. These fine gentlemen will recognize their contributions to my professional life in the pages of the revision of GROUP LEADERSHIP.

K.B.